D1431107

"In gripping detail, Karpowitz offers a human-driven account of efforts to reestablish higher education in America's prisons. Along the way, we're faced with the moral challenge: by what right do we restrict access to the country's best innovations to those who languish in its most barbarous?"

—Glenn E. Martin, founder and president, Just Leadership USA

"*College in Prison* is a deeply thoughtful meditation on one of the most pressing issues related to the US mass incarceration crisis: the inimitable, invaluable power of higher education behind bars. Karpowitz approaches this vital subject with the sensitivity of a practitioner and the meticulous analysis of a scholar, producing a worthy study that speaks to hearts and minds both."

—Baz Dreisinger, author of
Incarceration Nations: A Journey to Justice in Prisons Around the World

"This is a book for our time. It firmly plants college access as a core aspect in the prison reform agenda and infuses that agenda with humanity and hope. Karpowitz describes the teachers and students with kindness and honesty so that we see real people struggling to breathe the life of curiosity and engagement into the soul-killing place that prison can too often be. If you care about prison reform, this book will rock you."

—Todd R. Clear, author of *Imprisoning Communities*

"*College in Prison* is an absolutely unforgettable story of how and why an ambitious program at a relatively small New York–based academic institution might hold the key to a revolutionary way of reimagining our nation's approach to mass incarceration. Karpowitz has written a wonderfully sophisticated and moving story about his choice to devote the bulk of his adult life to a powerful project that takes prisoners and their possible futures incredibly seriously. Reading this text closely means never thinking about the implications of imprisonment quite the same way again."

—John L. Jackson Jr., dean, School of Social Policy and Practice,
University of Pennsylvania

"The Bard Prison Initiative has been a rare ray of light in the darkness of mass incarceration. Karpowitz's account tells its story, and turns that light to uncovering new truths about the American prison in our time."

—Jonathan S. Simon, author of *Mass Incarceration on Trial*

"Total praise for *College in Prison*! Karpowitz provides an argument that education helps to relieve the harm caused by incarceration. This work delivers an intimate glimpse into the hearts and minds of those for whom critical thinking has become salvation."

—Vivian Nixon, executive director,
College and Community Fellowship

"This gripping firsthand account of progressive pedagogy in prison at the height of mass incarceration by a dedicated scholar-activist and gifted educator is a truly inspiring and practical call to action to undo the brutality of our nation's lock-down."

—Philippe Bourgois, author of
In Search of Respect: Selling Crack in El Barrio

"Using his fascinating experiences with the Bard Prison Initiative, Daniel Karpowitz presents a refreshing take on pressing academic and social questions. This is an important story to tell."

—Joshua M. Price, author of *Prison and Social Death*

College in Prison

College in Prison

READING IN AN AGE OF
MASS INCARCERATION

DANIEL KARPOWITZ

RUTGERS UNIVERSITY PRESS
New Brunswick, New Jersey, and London

Library of Congress Cataloging-in-Publication Data
Names: Karpowitz, Daniel, author.
Title: College in prison : reading in an age of mass incarceration / Daniel
    Karpowitz.
Description: New Brunswick, New Jersey : Rutgers University Press,
    2017. | Includes bibliographical references and index.
Identifiers: LCCN 2016012331| ISBN 9780813584126 (hardback)
    | ISBN 9780813584133 (e-book (epub)) | ISBN 9780813584140
    (e-book (web pdf))
Subjects: LCSH: Prisoners—Education (Higher)—New York (State)—
    History. | Education, Higher—Social aspects—New York (State)—
    History. | Prison administration—New York (State)—History. |
    Bard College—History. | BISAC: SOCIAL SCIENCE / Penology.
    | EDUCATION / Higher. | SOCIAL SCIENCE / Criminology. |
    EDUCATION / Philosophy & Social Aspects.
Classification: LCC HV8888.3.U62 N75 2017 | DDC
    365/.66609747—dc23
LC record available at https://lccn.loc.gov/2016012331

A British Cataloging-in-Publication record for this book is available from
the British Library.

Visit our website: http://rutgerspress.rutgers.edu

Manufactured in the United States of America

To my parents, who encouraged me to take what I had inherited and make it my own.

CONTENTS

Introduction

College inside prison creates new choices, new and alternative ways of being, that lie between the extremes of compliance and disobedience, between resistance and surrender.

Sandy-haired Peter Bay sat across from me, silent and stiff, his face purged of expression. The flatness of his gaze offered no clue as to what he wanted to say or how much he felt was at stake. He was a white, working-class man in his mid-thirties who had dropped out of school in the ninth grade and had completed the high-school equivalency exam in prison.

He and I and the other interviewer sat face to face at the admissions interviews for the college we represented. We sat in a clinical, brightly lit classroom near the back of the hundred-acre, maximum-security prison compound. The tinny acoustics made each spoken exchange feel distant, although we sat directly across from each other on either side of a small table. Mr Bay had applied in each of the two previous years and had been rejected both times. He was in pursuit of something he wanted deeply, in an environment starved of opportunity. This was his third application in as many years, and it was not going well.

Like many applicants, Mr Bay had worked his way from prison to prison across the state specifically to get himself to a location where he could apply to the college. For, although our college had built six different satellite campuses in prison, these were almost the only such places left after Congress eliminated college from America's prisons in the mid-1990s. Many men sweat heavily when writing their timed application essays, and later, when they sit for their interview. They search, with little clue, for what they think "the college" wants to hear, and grapple with how honest to be about their ambitions, misgivings, and suspicions. Despite operating under such extraordinarily difficult conditions, most applicants speak profusely, generating a lively exchange in their interview with the college representative they're meeting, almost always for the first time.

Mr Bay, however, barely spoke. He didn't sweat, he didn't confront, and he certainly didn't try to charm. His mouth was parched, and he tried to moisten his lips repeatedly without success. He spoke in heavy, awkward measures as if his words were being dislodged one at a time. When he did speak, I heard a mid-Atlantic, working-class white accent with a colonial-era twang that sounded a lot like that of my mother, who had grown up in a post-industrial shipping district along the Delaware River. As he halted and censored himself throughout the interview, he made, for the third year in a row, a very unconvincing case for admission.

His stillness suggested an intense effort at self-control. I knew his face as well as his application file from the previous two years. Once again he was among a hundred men competing for fifteen spots in the incoming class of Bard College inside the Eastern Correctional Facility, a maximum-security prison in upstate New York, an hour's drive from the Bard campus. Yet again he had written a lackluster—in fact, a barely competent—essay and, although among the forty to be chosen for an interview, he was once again on track to be denied.

A huge floor fan whirred deafeningly in the far corner, drowning out our voices but barely moving the stale, heavy air. Noises from the prison yard ricocheted in through the armored windows and rattled around the bare walls and tiled floor.

He took a breath.

"I have never—" he broke off—"I have never wanted anything like this before." I waited for more, but that was all.

"Mr Bay," I said. "It is clear that you want this and it matters a lot to us that you do. We pay no attention to GED scores, and try to disregard the familiar battery of diagnoses about student deficits. Desire and seriousness of purpose mean a lot. We don't want to waste an opportunity that's precious on someone who doesn't really give a damn, on someone not really committed to doing the work." I continued, "Your sincerity, the strength of your desire can carry you a long way. This college is really hard, and most people might not have your kind of determination to manage, to forge ahead with the work, to confront their own limitations and put up with ours. . . ."

From Bay, more silence, not dead, but rather faltering.

I could talk a bit more, I thought, giving him time to collect his thoughts under the cover of someone else's chatter. I continued.

"But wanting it really badly can't be—or let's say it isn't, in our case—all that we consider. Let's assume many guys want it badly, and that all of them are more or less sincere. We can't get too hung up on our own impressions of sincerity—least of all in here, under these conditions. But it does matter greatly that someone will make the most of the opportunity, and will find something in common in their ambitions and ours."

Bay nodded, listening. I hoped it was obvious that I was trying above all to buy him time.

"Look," I said, "people can simply write their way into the college—just on the strength of their essay alone. That's because reading those texts, the prompts we give—the Du Bois, the Tocqueville, the Adrienne Rich—whatever—reading them and writing those essays in response to them—that sort of thing actually stands pretty well for a lot of what we actually *do* in the college."

Now he was looking at me, listening rather than struggling for his own words.

"Mr Bay, I don't want you to walk out of this interview and feel that there were things you had wanted to say but forgot under the pressure. We have plenty of time."

We did not, of course. There were rooms up and down the prison hallway full of people waiting to interview.

"Your essay, Peter, as you probably kind of know, showed that you might be able to do that sort of work. That's why—well, frankly, that's why you keep getting interviews. This is your third, isn't it?"

"My second," he said. "Two years ago I didn't get an interview."

I paused and let him continue; he seemed not to be searching for the right words, but to be silencing those that came to mind.

"Well, your essays show it, Mr Bay, but you're not offering us much beyond that. Writing like that, *reading* like it—it's a very difficult thing to do—it's a practice—by which I mean it's a habit and a skill that has to be acquired. A beautiful one—you'll enjoy it eventually. What you do with your mind, and your heart, when you really *read* someone else; what it takes to move your thoughts and feelings into writing . . . none of that is 'natural,' it doesn't *come* naturally. You have to learn how to do it." I paused. "Your essay has promise, it has gotten you an interview—"

"The last two times," he added, a smile mixing self-criticism and accusation. Surely there was much he might justifiably say to accuse us of being inscrutable in our demands, opaque in our preferences, capricious in our decisions. I waited, hoping he might say more.

"Obviously," I added thoughtlessly, defensively, "spaces in the college are scarce—"

And I was the one to interrupt himself this time. It's cowardly when people in any authority invoke scarcity to justify their actions. I was going to form a judgment and make a decision, both of which would be my own. And I had to own up, along with my colleagues, to the shortcomings of our admissions process. We were committed to keeping each incoming cohort small enough so as to engage them with the level of academic rigor and individualized study that is typical of a college like Bard. Of course, if "scarcity" were truly a first principle, we wouldn't be sitting there in a maximum-security prison trying to run a first-rate liberal arts college with students who could never afford to pay, and with no public financial support whatsoever. *Scarcity is the beginning of justice*, David Hume had said, and I always felt that to be wrong. Very concise, very intuitive, and very wrong.

I tried again. "Mr Bay, the group of us that read the essay—there's a whole crew of us on campus, faculty, staff, etc., as you know . . . each of us reads each of these essays. Five people read a hundred, sometimes two hundred essays, ranking them in private, discussing them around the table. It's quite a chore; though it can be fun and is always, once or twice a year, inspiring. Anyway, we can usually agree on four, maybe five that seem really ready, or really promising, or obviously worth the risk. We ask ourselves, *Are they reading the text? Do they understand it? Can they pay attention, really, to the words of the author before them? Do they write something that is insightful or attentive? Can they write a solid sentence? A paragraph? Is there a composition here?* That sort of thing.

"But really," I said, "beyond four or five essays—out of say a hundred—beyond that, there's a lot of guesswork. But we've decided to replicate the process of getting into a high-quality, selective college—so as not to create something in the prison that's so completely different from how it works 'out there,' on the main campus. And that's also why we have these interviews. The point here is to give applicants an extra chance to say something relevant, interesting, insightful, something of their own. About the text maybe. About college. About reading, or even the jails. God knows it can be easier to talk than to write."

He nodded gravely.

I was repeating things I'd heard myself say a hundred times before. Bay tried to moisten his lips. I resisted looking up at the clock, or down at my wrist. We were out of time.

"Right," I went on, "So we understand that the college may be a mystery to you. You haven't been to one before; you got your GED inside. That's fine. Coming to college is supposed to be a discovery." I cringed hearing this. I had run out of things to say, but I went on. "Finding out what it is, and how it might matter to you, how it might be or become important to certain parts of you."

He nodded slightly, listening intently, and waited.

"Why *this*, Mr Bay? Why the college?"

"They," he broke in, "they have . . ." and he stopped.

"Look, Peter. I don't work here. I and the other faculty are here as guests of the Department of Corrections, and we try to be the best guests possible. But our employer is the college, and our calling comes as teachers and scholars, and during admissions we're here in search of new students. Speak your mind."

"They have their own ideas of rehabilitation," he said.

I looked at him and raised my eyebrows in invitation.

"Who are 'they'"? I asked.

"Yes," Bay answered, licking his dry lips to no effect, speaking slowly. "I can see why you would ask me that. It sounds like I mean the whole world when I say that."

And for an instant, a real smile seemed to break out across his face.

"By 'they' I mean the people here, who run this place. The COs—the correctional officers—the civilian staff."

For what seemed like the first time that morning, Bay was listening to himself and imagining how he sounded to somebody else, he was imagining me as a listener. He was not merely "self-conscious" and self-censoring, but more than that, he was thinking in a way oriented outward, to me, to the college.

He continued. "I suppose when I say 'they' it's a way of referring not just to this or that person, but to 'the system.'" He made the gesture for scare-quotes.

"You know, Mr Bay, I always ask who 'they' are. Once a student laughed at me and answered: 'Well, when I was growing up, 'they' was everybody beyond 55th and Flatbush.' And so I asked him 'So, who is it now?' And he grew sober and said, 'The prison.'"

We paused there for a moment, and then I spoke again.

"What we take for granted is revealing. I listen to myself—I keep an ear out—for whenever I myself use the word 'they'—and I always learn something about what it was I was thinking, what I was taking for granted, when I said it."

Bay nodded, but his smile disappeared, and he added gravely, "You can tell where a man thinks he is. Where he thinks he can go," he paused, "and where he thinks he can't."

I looked at him expectantly, waiting for more.

"Our sense of the boundaries . . . the limits between 'us' and 'them,'" he went on.

"Why do you use the scare quotes, Mr Bay?" I asked, making the gesture with my fingers in the air as I spoke. His decision to do that interested me greatly, but he seemed to ignore the question.

"What we feel lies within our control," he went on, "and not."

I nodded. "It may be worth noting too," I offered, "that there's always a hypothesis, inside our minds, an implicit theory, about who 'they' are and what 'their' motives, powers, and interests are."

He nodded, as if waiting to hear more. I said nothing.

Bay added: "Our use of the word says as much about *us* as it does about 'them.'"

I frowned, with my eyebrows raised, as a sign of appreciation. I quite liked that idea. Then there was a long silence again, and he gave no sign of going on. I tried to pick up an earlier thread.

"You were saying that they have their own ideas of rehabilitation?"

"You're expected to be obedient," he went on, "not just to conform only, I mean not just to, you know, follow the basic rules of living in society, to try and make yourself a better person (whatever they think *that* means, I mean I have my own ideas, very much so)—but . . ."

He trailed off and then resumed.

"I want it to be about living different, finding out *how* in the hell you can live different, for the first time in your life . . . find . . . who you should be. But . . ."

"But?"

"Too often it just becomes about someone trying to get you, to force you, to do what they say."

For the first time it was easy to look at him, and I in turn felt easier having him look at me, sitting in front of him as a representative of the college, deciding on admissions without embarrassment.

"It's not *about* anything in here," he went on. "It seems to me . . . It's just a . . . It's just about humiliation. It's not corrections—that's what they call it. 'Corrections.' It's not—" he broke off and fell silent, his thin lips immobile again, and cold. I guessed that the missing word he had halted at was "rehabilitation." He seemed not to want to say it, to use it to describe what went on in there.

I tried to appear neutral, for I agreed with him perhaps too much.

"That's what it means to them." He started again, stopped, and resumed. "I know. I need—to change." He stopped again. "My life. The college. Can be different."

He put the pieces out there, and then he strung it together. "It's a different way. Not their way. Something else. I *know* I need it. Of course I do. Look at me. Look at what I've made of everything. But I could do that. It could be a way for me. I know it could."

I said nothing.

"I have never pursued anything like this before," he said. "Never put myself out there for . . . for something I really wanted. Nothing has ever mattered to me like this."

Bay fell silent.

He had come full circle and we were out of time.

I later learned that Bay was incarcerated since his early twenties for what seemed, based on the record, a nonviolent and mid-level crime. He'd already served a long bid for that kind of charge. I assume that his case, like that of so many others, involved a plea bargain or, more accurately, his refusal to bargain. And so the book, as they say, had been thrown at him. It is ironic that one reason American justice is so harsh is because it's so democratic—or at least populist. One of the most democratic features of our system is the breadth of discretionary power given to locally elected prosecutors—district attorneys—who channel popular passion and opinion directly into the administration of the criminal law. We don't have a civil service of professional prosecutors, with expertise in cost-benefit analysis or risk management, insulated from the daily tides of popular opinion. It's telling that the only true tribunes of the people we have in our political system are the prosecutors who run the front end of our systems of punishment.

At the level of daily life in prison, Bay seemed prepared to submit to the basic rules and codes of behavior. If not, he would have been moved out of a relatively peaceful prison like Eastern to somewhere harsher, or more rigid, and with fewer programs, typically farther upstate. But Bay had been telling me that he was not prepared to fully submit to the inner logic of the prison or the morality that he thought animated many of its demands. He desired a change for himself, but at the same time he opposed many features of the moral machinery charged with his "correction." *Its* discourse of rehabilitation and *its* practices of correction seemed to him to threaten, rather than facilitate, his own desire for change.

I believe that students who apply to the college inside realize that an effort like BPI is in fact a collaboration, often a very close one, between the college and some of the prison's staff and leadership. Indeed, resentment of this collaboration may keep many people in prison from ever applying. Bay was no doubt aware of the cooperation between the two institutions, but he was even more drawn to the gulf that he sensed between them. I understood him to be saying that to enroll in the college was not merely to fight against the system, but to transform his daily life into a struggle that could be won here and now, and that served the purposes about which he felt most strongly.

In an instant, Bay had clarified for me what for years I had only intuited: that the college is important in part because it presents definitions of participation and modes of conformity that differed from those of the prison. In the broadest view, this is why I feel the college inside the prison is an important *political* space, with implications for the nation at large, even as we work to reduce our generation's overuse of prisons. I have also come to learn, from a vantage point so different from his, that many professionals and officials within corrections think that it is entirely within the public mission of prison systems to cultivate, inside prisons, alternative ways of being, with alternative modes of discipline, dignity, and respect.

Bay spoke to me of this with yearning, and articulated a clear understanding of the work that I myself had long sought. His initial vagueness, his struggle for clarity, suggested that he was being drawn toward something unlike anything he had known before. As I understood it, his sense was that by getting himself into the college he would join in a rigorous discipline that he himself would help create; that in the college he might find the way to participate in a system without giving in to it. This means to join with others, perhaps for the first time, in building something vulnerable but resilient, and something that can only be made, and understood, in common.

Later that day we admitted Mr Bay to the college.

WHEN I WAS a student of constitutional law I learned a lesson that for me is a bridge to the political significance of establishing an independent liberal arts college inside a prison. Victor Osiatynski is a Polish human rights lawyer who was involved in writing a new constitution for his country after Poland gained its independence from the Soviet Union in 1989. I met him while I was in law school at the University of Chicago, where he was a regular visiting professor. Short, with a round belly and rosy cheeks, he wore a gold signet ring set with a tiny ruby on his pinky finger. The theme of Victor's seminar was the question: "What defines constitutional government?" and he had a surprising answer. It is not, he argued, the separation of powers, or a rule of laws not persons, or any of the things we were used to being taught.

"Rather," Victor argued, "constitutionalism is that form of politics that creates as many options as possible *that are neither submission nor rebellion.* A constitutional regime takes these two points and opens up a space between them, as wide a space as possible. This implies," Victor concluded, "that tyranny collapses the range of differences, leaving people with a frightening but quite simple choice: you either transgress, or you obey."

For me, this is the primary significance of what Peter Bay said when he was applying to study with Bard at Eastern. He sought a way forward, through the institutions of punishment, not to avoid his own responsibilities in life, but rather to embrace them with dignity. This, too, says much about the dramas played out by so many others represented in the pages that follow.

I've come to believe that much of what BPI does—as a liberal arts college—is to open up these spaces where the range of what is appropriate is broadened. There, our urges to praise, to condemn, or to solve a problem are deferred, and as a result, judgment flourishes by becoming more complex and more self-conscious. With Victor's reasoning about constitutional regimes in mind, and the highest regard for the republican roots of America's own political culture, this form of learning and socializing takes on additional significance in the landscape of the prison. It is one reason why, as discussed in depth below, the liberal arts education is actually in no need of alteration when it is taken up inside such a setting: the contrast it presents to the tendencies of the governing institutional regime are already pervasive and profound.

If there's any element of truth in this characterization of the college, then it resembles the sort of practice my old teacher of constitutionalism was talking about, where the proliferation of questions, challenges, and revisions is not conceived as rebellion, but as a form of participation and respect. In lieu of compliance, or obedience, one is called to contribute to the creation of a larger, common institution, the college, by way of the cultivation and embellishment of the self.

It is a way of engaging and confronting the authorities that we encounter in the world around us, and those that we hear— and interrogate—within ourselves.

A Note on the Text

This book is an extended reflection on what has been my calling for much of the past two decades: the building of college-in-prison programs, originally and most extensively the Bard Prison Initiative (BPI) in New York. Over the years, I have worked alongside a team of extraordinary partners, including all of the students, the program's lead founder and executive director, and, more recently, with colleagues in academia, philanthropy, and state agencies across the country. The contributions of students and colleagues are everywhere and deep, although the flaws, misjudgments, and inaccuracies that follow are entirely my own.

Many scenes are re-creations of moments inside prison, drawn from my experiences as both a teacher working with students and as an administrator working with colleagues in both the academy and state governments. Everyone is presented with a pseudonym. The re-creations of conversations are drawn from memory but based on extensive journals and files that I have kept over a period spanning much of the fifteen years I have done the work. Many of these journals are written, while others were recorded on micro-cassettes during the long drives to and from work; these have been supplemented by authorized videos of graduations.

The College remains in touch with hundreds of students who have since returned home. Of those students depicted at any length here, however, I am in contact with only one. He has seen and read through the manuscript and commented extensively on its drafts at several formative moments. His insights and judgments that informed the final version have been of inestimable value to me as an author, and they only add to the debt I owe him. The final text has also benefited immeasurably from the constructive if sometimes withering criticism of some of the people who know the field best and think most deeply about it, including several academic colleagues: Megan Callaghan, Craig Wilder, Ellen Lagemann, and Laura Kunreuther. The many faults that clearly remain despite their best efforts are, of course, entirely my own.

Finally, numerous parts of this book serve as a description of BPI itself: a specific and highly complex institution. I had nothing to do with the initial conception and founding of BPI, which was largely done by Max Kenner and his colleagues at Bard in the late 1990s. From the outset, BPI has been a richly collaborative creation of numerous professors, instructors, administrators, and students, and this collective creativity has only increased with the breadth of BPI's endeavors and the diverse achievements of its faculty and alumni. I have taught and helped design and build BPI since its very first semester. Having made it my primary vocation for the better part of two decades, and, as director of policy and academics, I have been instrumental in forming most of its core features. While I am well situated to speak to some of what I believe are its mechanics and significance, I do not write on behalf of BPI, its leadership, or the myriad creative and courageous people who make it a living reality.

College in Prison

"America—a country devoted to the death of paradox."
—James Baldwin, "Many Thousands Gone"

CHAPTER 1

Getting In

CONFLICTING VOICES AND
THE POLITICS OF COLLEGE IN PRISON

COLLEGE IN PRISON is offensive. When hard-working people struggle to pay their kids' tuition and people carry more debt for college than on their credit cards, handing the guilty a free education is an outrage. Commit a crime and get a free education? We ought to reward those who play by the rules and punish those who don't.

THE AMERICAN RATE of imprisonment has increased 500 percent since 1980 and the money spent on staffing prisons has increased over 400 percent. Totaling about 80 billion dollars a year, state spending on prisons now often exceeds budgets for higher education. Some unions for prison staff complain of the rising cost of college for their kids, but fall silent on the role their own sector has played in drawing money away from public investments in education.

Creating college opportunity inside is inexpensive and its fiscal benefits are large. Almost everyone who goes to college while in prison is released—and almost none of them ever go back. Populist critics rarely object to the millions spent on non-college "programs" in prison: therapies, boot camps, evangelical "character building," and other techniques of behavioral modification. It may be the dignity or social status of higher education alone that provokes resentment, not the money it costs. We should be working to make college affordable and accessible for all Americans, rather than pretending that keeping it away from people in prison does anybody else any good.

PRISON SHOULD BE a place where bad people are sent to suffer for the wrongs they have done to others. Our success in lowering crime has come through increased policing, harsher sentences, and expanded prisons. This toughness works—but it's also a sign of moral integrity. After the excesses of the 1960s and the failures of the welfare state, Americans have regained their nerve. We no longer tolerate whining about how criminals are the victims of circumstance or inequality or racism. Crime is down because punishment is up. The desire for revenge, which makes liberals cringe, is rooted in human nature and our religious traditions. Putting college in prison makes it seem that "society," rather than individual men and women, are responsible for the crimes they have committed: it's a sign of moral weakness and of backsliding toward the failed, liberal sentimentality of the past.

MASS INCARCERATION IS "the New Jim Crow." A college that enters today's prison system becomes the handmaiden of something irredeemably corrupt. Out "on the street," liberal arts colleges are bastions of class and racial privilege. When they step inside a prison to help a fraction of those confined there, they provide a fig-leaf for a system that should instead be abolished.

One in three African American men will spend part of their lives behind bars. An African American child born today is six times more likely to go to prison than the white child born nearby, and blacks are disproportionately stopped, arrested, and incarcerated in every state in the U.S. Notoriously, California has at times gone so far as to plan future prison-building by counting the number of poor children of color in their elementary schools.

The leaders of America's systems of higher education are often passive bystanders to the broader structural inequality of which mass incarceration is only a part. Colleges and universities that have failed to make American higher education adequately equal and accessible cannot absolve themselves by making gestures on behalf of a handful of incarcerated blacks. On entering the country's carceral factories, the country's privileged and largely white academic institutions can only serve to make the madness seem acceptable, reformable, reformed.

To make matters worse, the implicit message of college in prison—that hard work and individual discipline can make bad people better—strengthens the logic of punishment and the illusion that American laws are color-blind and fair. Under such conditions, the "liberal arts" become a caricature, offering "transformation" to the wayward convict. Prisons—along with the self-satisfied educational reformers within them—should be swept away.

Saul Bellow was right when he mockingly declared that "education has become the great and universal American recompense. It has even replaced punishment in the federal penitentiaries. . . . The tigers of wrath are crossed with the horses of instruction, making a hybrid undreamed of in the Apocalypse."

College and prison cannot—and must not—be reconciled.

EACH OF THE above statements represents a real-world view of education inside our prisons that I have encountered in the past fifteen years. These views contradict each other, but none is entirely wrong.

College in prison awakens lurking doubts about whether anybody ever truly changes—a question that lies at the heart of nearly all thinking not only about education, but also about democracy itself. My aim is neither to please my natural supporters nor to persuade the skeptics. In writing this book I have tried to avoid becoming an advocate, despite the fact that I think we should clearly be doing more to provide liberal arts college in prison. As often as

possible I've tried to draw out the complexities inherent in the
work. Nearly all of the students the college has engaged in prison
are guilty of serious crimes, most of them violent crimes. (Otherwise fully justified critics of mass incarceration have an unfortunate
tendency to ignore or minimize the ethical and political complexity that arises from violent crime.) On the other hand, I see most
forms of punishment as unfortunate mirror-images of the violence
to which they respond. All of the prisons I have entered strike me
as places of waste that perpetuate and intensify both racial and class
inequality. As a result, prisons, among the most important and pervasive public institutions of our age, undermine our democracy and
do a disservice to the republic they are meant to serve.

When students first enroll with the college inside prison,
they are often well aware that what we are doing together is controversial. They may not yet appreciate, however, just how many
avid supporters of college and post-secondary education there
are among people who work within corrections, among public officials and career civil servants, and persistently among the
broader public as well. Yet they are by and large acutely aware that
many people do resent or oppose such opportunities for people
in prison. Strikingly, in my experience, students in prison are often
remarkably perceptive about such critiques. They understand and
partially share some of the reasoning behind them, and are often
sympathetic to them—despite their own personal pursuit of the
opportunity and their advocacy on behalf of it as a matter of principle and policy.

Such students undertake a personal struggle to rekindle or
realize their own long-deferred or thwarted ambitions, and they
commit to caring for and building something precious, despite
being surrounded by an institution that mostly evokes resistance,
cynicism, and alienation. They explore new forms of empowerment inside a system they may reject, in its practice if not
its premise. These are burdens that almost no conventional student ever faces. Indeed, the very circumstances that confront the

student in prison often lead to a greater awareness of the stakes involved in pursuing education, and a more profound fulfillment of liberal learning's promise by a wider range of students. Remaining sensitive to these burdens, while encouraging students to nevertheless challenge themselves and live up to their full potential, to take possession of their own talents and responsibility for their own cultivation, is one of the great challenges facing all who work or teach in this field. It is a challenge that many students deeply perceive and appreciate even before they have begun their formal studies. These conditions make the academic and personal achievements of students in prison all the more remarkable; they also deepen, rather than compromise, the importance of the liberal arts as a mode of education acutely relevant to the prison and students within it.

Americans have vastly diverse opinions about college in prison, as they have about crime and punishment broadly. Some believe that educating inmates is a powerful rehabilitative tool; others feel that jail must be a place of pain and deprivation. To exacerbate the issue, mass incarceration is a deeply racialized phenomenon, while college has become increasingly unaffordable for all working- and middle-class Americans regardless of where they live or the subject positions into which they have been formed.

Moral sentiments often trace divisions of race and class. They reveal divergent attitudes not only toward crime and punishment, but also toward the arts, humanities, history, literature, and science—in short, to the entire project of liberal education. At times, many simply hold such things in contempt, considering them suspiciously effete or elitist, or worse.

THE VIEWS EXPRESSED about people in prison and the idea of college inside amount to arguments for and against what has been my career for a decade and a half: building networks of liberal arts colleges running inside prison. The Bard Prison Initiative, based at Bard College in New York, operates satellite campuses inside state prisons across the state. Three hundred incarcerated men and women go to Bard College full-time inside prison. They earn Bard credits and both AA and BA degrees. For the past several years we have also worked with other colleges and universities to forge similar programs of their own, in partnerships with allies in state government.

BPI's students are demographically identical to the general population of the prisons within which we work. Yet the education they seek through BPI, and at which they flourish at such high levels, is usually the privilege of elites only. Such educational forms are defined by training in rigorous methods across many disciplines (humanistic, scientific, sociological), a principled commitment to the questioning of convention and received wisdom, and a devotion to the empowerment and transformation of the self through critical inquiry.

In the fall of 2001 Max Kenner invited me to join the faculty in the first semester of Bard's offering college courses in prison. Max had led a group of Bard college students who had founded BPI two years earlier. Students organized whatever resources they could inside the prison—lectures, writing workshops, participation in theology seminars—but their aim was always to draw the college into offering its degree to people in prison. These undergrads, some privileged and some not, shared a sense that they could take some responsibility for how the college engaged with the world. In their eyes, the college could do its part to fill the great void left after Bill Clinton signed the Crime Control Act of 1994, a law that directed billions of federal dollars toward building more prisons, while making people inside them immediately ineligible for Pell grants.

Pell grants had made a huge impact inside American prisons. Higher education quickly became the most efficient, affordable, and effective "program" in American corrections, consistently associated with the lowest rates of recidivism—meaning people who went to college while incarcerated almost never came back to prison again. It was stunningly cheap: at their peak, in 1994, such programs nationally cost a total of one half of one percent of all Pell spending. Yet in 1995, Congress not only made people in prison ineligible for Pell grants, but also appropriated ten billion dollars of taxes to build more prisons.

Perhaps because of the ways privilege and inequality often mingled in New York City and at Bard in the 1990s, these students were keenly aware that young people from the city followed two divergent pathways coming and going "upstate." Some were moving up for the privilege of attending colleges like Bard; many more were moved up to serve sentences that were being imposed more often, and lasting longer, than ever before. Though the phrase "mass incarceration" had not yet gained much currency, these students were among those who realized relatively early that criminal justice was emerging as the leading civil rights issue of their generation. Most importantly, they felt strongly that returning college to the prisons that lay a short drive from campus in nearly every direction was the kind of practical, local work that they, as students, could help make happen, and that would mobilize the best of what the college had to offer.

The students began cultivating relationships with prison officials and potential students, at the nearby maximum security facility called "Eastern." A few years earlier, many of these partners had been a part of college programs before they were suddenly shut down. Many public officials—now operating in a hostile political climate—remained deeply committed to helping such opportunities return.

When I first stepped foot inside Eastern Correctional Facility to teach, I was overwhelmed by the century-old, gothic-style, maximum-security prison. I was silenced by its massive physical and spiritual presence. I felt a sense of tragedy, knowing that prisons (which in New York had grown from twenty-five to more than seventy in just a few years) were the signature public works of our generation.

But my reaction to the students, and the classroom space inside the prison, was quite different. The students were just students, and my course was just my course, and, at that early stage of my career, I especially loved teaching, anybody and anywhere. Once I walked into the classroom and the heavy metal door closed behind me, I began my introductory lecture about constitutional history and the entwined nineteenth-century problems of slavery and territorial expansion. It was the same course in law and the humanities, focused on the antebellum period, that I had taught two years earlier at Berkeley. The students, intent and committed, threw themselves into the problems of the class and the knotty tasks of interpreting and reinterpreting the texts. For me as a teacher, nothing could have seemed more natural and familiar as our journey through the material.

To this day, the approach to a prison building and the journey through its labyrinth of hallways are oppressive experiences. I am no more immune to the depressing panorama of a large prison today than I was fifteen years ago. (Most difficult for me personally is witnessing the children of people in prison passing through the gates to visit their parents.) But the classroom spaces themselves, created wherever I have the pleasure of joining students in their college work, remain as gratifying as any good learning encounter anywhere. It can be very difficult to convince professors to come inside a prison to teach a class. But once they do, they almost inevitably want to come back and do it again, and again. For it is in such classrooms, and with such students, that they are reminded of what they once loved about teaching. No doubt the logistical challenges of getting from a campus and into the prison classroom dramatize the moral and political significance of doing the work. They also heighten professors' sense of the value of what they do. But above all, it is the students in prison who make the experience acute. They have endured the fact and conditions of their incarceration, and they have taken myriad personal risks to apply. Confronting their own past failures and broken ambitions, they must have already resolved to find opportunity in their confinement. In the face of great symbolic and material oppressiveness, these students enter college with the keenest sense of just how precious is the opportunity that lies before them.

BPI is a part of Bard College and replicates as much as possible of the curriculum and academic culture on the main campus. All students work toward Bard AA and BA degrees in the liberal arts. Courses of study include anthropology, literature, science, politics, history, studio arts—with the full intensity of what a college like Bard demands of its students. All majors are declared through an intensive, portfolio-based process called "moderation." All students receive grades, along with qualitative narrative reports, for each class. The curriculum includes mandatory trainings in specific preparatory units like "Language and Thinking," "Citizen Science," and a sequence of First Year Seminars. Nearly all remediation is woven into the heart of the main, academic curriculum. Mathematics runs from precollege algebra through the full calculus sequence, although dozens of students in prison now major in mathematics, in a sequence that begins after Calculus III. Our first foreign languages, in which dozens of students have achieved proficiency or beyond, were Spanish, German, and Mandarin. Every BA degree must culminate in a yearlong intensive senior thesis. Extracurricular activities include visiting lectures by leading faculty from around the country and, most famously, the debate union, which competes with peer institutions such as West Point, the University of Vermont, and Harvard.

I have sought to draw an analogy between how Bard has approached college in prison, how I have tried to write this book, and how the most successful of our students have sought to refashion their lives. BPI has refused to make incarceration, or resistance to it, a guide to curriculum or pedagogy. Similarly, it has rejected the prison, and the correctional enterprise, as the measures of its success or failure. I see a strong parallel between this approach, the achievement of so many of our students, and my own aspiration in writing about them both. I have attempted to do what many of the students have done in the course of their lives—to resist cliché, the imagery that constitutes us, and yet which we, in turn, refashion. This is exactly what I think Mr Bay was doing in his interview: rejecting the clichés inherent in the system that confined him while avoiding other clichés to describe his own insistent search for an alternative way forward.

Every "student" depicted in the pages that follow is also an "inmate," "offender," or "prisoner," in their own eyes or in the eyes of those surrounding them. In no small part, the struggles around these contested and competing identities define the milieu of the college in prison. The college's role, I believe, is extraordinarily complex in this encounter, since the academic challenge is paradoxical: to open a space where these contested identities can be recognized as well as transcended, critiqued, and escaped and transformed—but *without* becoming terms that define and limit the educational project. Above all, they must not be the terms on which the encounter between the college and its students first unfolds, and they must not be the wellspring of imagery or ambition that the college and its faculty brings to their students in prison.

At BPI, we seek to address the student in prison as we would any other student at a liberal arts college. The academic encounter is thus constructed as one that unfolds not because of the prison, but despite it. Each student enters the college about as "marked" or labeled as any student could possibly be; yet part of our job is to address them as we do others who are among the 1 percent of students who study at a private, liberal arts college. The college has tried to meet each student on terms so that the student's identity remains contingent and open to the idiosyncratic dynamics that follow from their own individual education.

Successful students in the college-in-prison programs, some of whom are portrayed in this book, have thrived in part because as thinkers and actors they have navigated the tropes within which they live about their past, about change, about choice. These tropes have great gravity, to which the prison and the apparatus of punishment and stigma add only greater weight. In becoming students in a liberal arts college they have embraced an additional identity and another framework that coexists along with the others. They have undertaken the work of remaking themselves and their understanding of the world around them, in and beyond the prison, with daily habits of discipline and critical engagement.

There are several dominant story lines about the work of college in prison. Public officials and correctional professionals often see education as a chrysalis of change that reforms the inmate and lowers recidivism. Alternatively, activist-scholars who enter the prison sometimes enact a romance in which they deploy a "pedagogy of the oppressed" and in which students and faculty, as comrades, speak truth to power, resisting the structures of race, class, or "governmentality." Conservative intellectuals, nostalgic for an age of supposedly disinterested intellectual inquiry and universal reasoning (before our "Fall" into the modern analysis of power and identity), may seek in the prison a haven in which the classics can cure the soul and prove yet again that freedom is a state of the mind, not the body. I would like to think that BPI has charted a path for the college and its students that avoids the pitfalls of each of these clichés.

Does going to college in prison change people? I am quite sure that it does, just as working in prison or being incarcerated in one, or attending any liberal arts college does. Any rich set of disciplines, personal transitions, and newly acquired networks will be transformative, altering people and the future trajectory of their lives. Indeed, at the heart of any educational endeavor is a belief that change is possible. This explains the central role that learning has always played in the democratic tradition. But ironically, in order for the potential of liberal education to survive the "instrumental" conditions of the prison and its complex of coercive machinery, our focus must lie elsewhere. If there is a connection between "change" and the justifications for college in prison, our foremost goal must be not to change people in prison, but to change the landscape of the prison itself.

PRISONS AND THE LIBERAL ARTS

For colleges and universities, doing this work is indeed about taking risks—but these risks are overwhelmingly moral and political, not physical. They involve having the institutional courage to seek out unconventional students with great promise, and to envision them as a central part of the academy's greatest intellectual and democratic ambitions.

In 2005, when BPI was several years old, we were invited by an organization of women incarcerated in New York City and their allies to open a Bard campus at Bayview, a prison on Tenth Avenue in Manhattan. There was no public money in the work and little to no prestige. Although raising private support for BPI was grueling, it was one of the many aspects of the work at which Max Kenner, BPI's founder, excelled. And we met a great deal of resistance within the academy about whether work of the highest quality could go on in prison. Not one of the wealthy, prestigious universities of New York City was interested in going into Bayview, and the public universities were still largely prohibited from doing so. BPI, located a hundred miles away, was eager to engage. We wanted to reach out to women students for the first time, to raise the profile of our work in Manhattan, and to capitalize on the faculty across New York City who could contribute if we just gave them a way to get inside.

Max and I gave a presentation in the prison gym to about two hundred incarcerated women who had gathered to hear what Bard had to offer. We were introduced by prison officials, but also by several women who helped create the opportunity. Women sat in rows of folding chairs, and we stood somewhat awkwardly at the front.

Not long into our presentation, an older woman asked, "Why is Bard interested in being here? What's in it for you?" Several heads nodded. Everyone was eager for an answer.

Max said that Bard was a fairly prestigious college and thought highly of itself—maybe a little more than was warranted, he joked—but that it was also neither as wealthy nor as prestigious as its competitors among the liberal arts colleges of the Northeast. "So we have to earn our reputation, and we're willing to take risks to do so. We are certain that there are great potential students in here, and in facilities around the state. We're determined to give them an opportunity to do the same kind of study that we have enjoyed ourselves."

"So you're out to earn a reputation on our backs?" she challenged, but with a smile.

"*With you*, I would say," answered Max. "To earn it together, and to our mutual benefit. Through the hard work and great fun of going to a really good, really ambitious college."

Some looked skeptical and others laughed. One applauded and shouted out, while others shook their heads.

We had several ways of introducing the college to prospective students in prison: our need to make a name for ourselves by taking risks others would not; and, alternatively, a tradition of creating liberal arts colleges in hostile environments, which I was about to turn to. As different as these explanations were, they shared an important factor: neither had anything to do with criminal justice, or helping people in prison, or lowering recidivism.

Max spoke up. "Bard has a principled tradition of starting up liberal arts colleges in places where there are none, in places where this kind of learning has been kept out, or thrown out, and where their presence might make a great deal of difference—to the students, and to the educational culture around them. So Bard started the first liberal arts college in the former Soviet Union, at Smolny in current-day St Petersburg, and established a liberal arts program in post-Apartheid South Africa at Wits, the leading research university in Johannesburg. It has launched and runs an early college high school as a New York City public school, at which students from all the boroughs can go and graduate with an AA degree from Bard. So you can think of BPI as in this broader tradition. The prison, in that context, is an accident, and not the primary reason we are here."

A young woman stood up and took hold of the wireless microphone that Max and I had avoided. Her voice shook, but she was firm and outspoken. Unlike the older women who had spoken up, she looked only about twenty years old and presented a Spanish New York accent.

"You're all clearly very satisfied with yourselves for being here," she said. "But what is the point? You talk about the liberal arts and all of those beautiful subjects—history, literature, philosophy. We are poor. We are women of color. What is the point of these fancy subjects for us? We don't have the family business to go back to, or the trust fund. We need job training, a plan for the future. We need career skills because we're going to have to make our own ways in the world, and often to take care of others, and we're going back to the same poor neighborhoods we came from. What can rich, white Bard College do to prepare us for the lives *we* have to live when we get out of here?"

There was no applause and no laughter—just a dead and serious silence.

Max turned to me and gestured as if to ask if I wanted to reply. I could tell he was impressed.

I did my best. "Maybe you're right," I said. "Bard has often flirted with running out of money, but it's also undeniably an institution of privilege supported by networks all sorts of wealth and access. I can't possibly presume to speak to you about what you need or to question your judgments about what is most important to you, here, now, and in the future. But I can say that I'm convinced that what we have to offer is of value to you. In part it's even valuable for the things you point out that you need, immediately, just to survive."

She raised her eyebrows and waited. As I gathered my thoughts, she smirked.

"At the very least Bard is *hard*. And because of that the skills you'd get studying with our faculty have real value: the college demands that you tackle totally new and really hard material, and master it. You learn one method or technique, understand its strengths and weaknesses, and then you learn another, weighing their relative merits. You'd have to manage your time under all of the pressures and obstacles you already face here every day, but in an environment, the college classroom, that is designed to feel and be as different as possible."

"And why is all of that better than job training, and parenting classes, which a lot of the women here could use, and actual jobs?"

"Maybe it's not better. But Bard doesn't do those things, and I simply can't offer it to you. And some experts who specialize in this sort of thing make a convincing case that the liberal arts, especially when done with great rigor and excitement, *are* in fact a great preparation for practical jobs in the real world. The flip side, they argue, is that overly narrow training doesn't actually prepare a person for the inevitable *changes* in jobs that the world, and the marketplace, will inevitably drive a person into sooner rather than later. The benefits of 'job training,' as it were, might be overstated."

She seemed unconvinced.

"That said," I continued, "the college does work to get its alumni access to jobs, and BPI is committed to doing that even more so for our graduates. But here's a pitch on behalf of the liberal arts: the diversity of subjects it offers is supposed to reflect the diversity of knowledge and method and critical passion that has been developed by women and men like you for a long time. This diversity of topics and disciplines represents a small part of a world that is very complex. And it represents the complexity of talents and abilities that lie inside you—inside each of us. The idea is that this belongs to you—it's part of the inheritance that's due to you, and to which you can and should contribute as well."

She was skeptical, to put it mildly. But despite that, she decided to linger. She and I continued speaking off to the side of the room as the gathering broke up into smaller groups. She told me her name was Sofia, and she shared a bit more about how frustrated she felt with the impoverished alternatives inside the prison, and how unprepared she felt for getting out. She also made it clear that she spoke on behalf of many women there, who often discussed these issues in heated conversations among themselves. Before we left, I said simply, "Try it. Maybe something better for you will come along, sooner than later, and I hope it does. For now, this is all we've got—it's what we do. If it's lousy and useless, you can drop it. But please do apply."

Sofia did apply, and in the blind process of essay writings she scored well. Max and another colleague interviewed her, and the committee admitted her, and she studied for several years with Bard until she was released. Soon afterward, she continued her BA at Bard's main campus, starting in economics and ending with a major in cultural anthropology. Her senior thesis involved, in part, a critique of the ways formerly incarcerated people are represented and deployed in advocacy for prison reform. For several years she rose through the ranks at a leading criminal justice reform project in New York City. Sofia has since said, "As a child growing up in Brooklyn, I always *knew* that I was going to end up in prison." Now working as a teacher, mentor, and organizer back in her old neighborhood, she has been admitted to PhD programs at Berkeley and Michigan, but she seems intent on going to law school instead.

A college like Bard can be part of the solution to the problems that Sofia pressed upon us, despite the fact that common sense and much of the current political fad prefer to ignore or undermine the liberal arts. The disparagement of the liberal arts in favor of narrower and supposedly more practical training often strikes me as more a matter of ideology and bias, rather than hard-bitten realism based on compelling evidence.

BPI alumni, who have studied liberal arts with great depth, breadth, and vigor, while not training in a specific field, are now flourishing in diverse fields, trades, and professions. Others, prior to release, have completed innovative post-liberal-arts forms of vocational training that we and partners have developed, and are flourishing in careers in those specific fields. This is not merely anecdotal: across the board, the post-release employment rates among BPI graduates are between 65 percent and 80 percent, suggesting a strong link between intensive, high-quality, and long-term liberal arts study and future success in the "workplace"—for a population of graduates that otherwise faces the *highest rates* of unemployment and lowered earnings even without the additional obstacles created by a period of incarceration.

These impressive outcomes are unlikely to be specific to BPI; in fact, they support some of the best professional research that challenges conventional wisdom on whether or not STEM (Science, Technology, Engineering, Math) or focused vocational training lead to better longer-term employment and earnings than the liberal arts. Most notably, BPI's outcomes fit into broader patterns identified by Peter Capelli, an expert on the public policy of employment and management at the University of Pennsylvania's Wharton School. Capelli's systematic research and BPI's direct experience over the past decade and a half suggest that the liberal arts, perhaps especially for a range of students currently incarcerated, can be an excellent preparation for future employment and careers. At the very least, such information suggests that the refusal to actively include ambitious liberal arts modes of learning as part of a systematic approach to education for adults in and leaving prison is a serious shortcoming based on questionable reasoning. These educational opportunities are enhanced when offered in partnership with selective institutions like Bard or comprehensive four-year public universities (like our partners at Minnesota State University).

When it comes to education, the liberal arts are the first to be disparaged—especially, it is crucial to emphasize—for students who are poor, ethnically diverse, and, of course, incarcerated. Is this a function of sound policy and prudent concern for their long-term welfare? Or is it a function of bias against both liberal learning and the poor, shared by popularly elected officials and many elite liberals? BPI students, at impressive rates, have prepared themselves for success in the marketplace precisely through their pursuit of rigorous liberal arts studies during and after prison. These benefits come in addition to the other personal, political, intellectual, and creative rewards that may come from such studies. Some of our alumni's most notable successes include careers in community health, epidemiology, and computer programming. But other graduates and alumni are flourishing in jobs in human resources and at upper-level management positions in private enterprise, in the trades, in small businesses, and in academia. One of Sofia's former classmates at the same prison, now a vice-president at a for-profit company, has helped to hire hired dozens of other BPI alumni, men and women, to work on the shop floor and in management.

The stark material realities that Sofia and others at Bayview knew so deeply and spoke about with such passion present a very real, indeed vast and entrenched network of problems confronting people driven into and coming out of prison. Also real are the ways that privilege and inequality distort what education looks like for different students, depending on who and where they are. In the view of those who have built BPI and are launching programs elsewhere inspired by this approach, there is too much emphasis in policy on "training," on vocational education for poor people generally and especially on education for people in and exiting prison. Worst of all, perhaps, is the related emphasis on short-term education focused on the final months of incarceration. In my view, this approach replicates the narrowing of opportunity that the prison itself embodies. It also squanders an otherwise important opportunity to engage students with the most meaningful, diverse forms of both empowering and creative education and practical preparation for a long and varied work life. In practice and in principle, BPI has attempted to break down the facile boundaries between "vocational" and "liberal arts" education. We do this by cultivating students' deepest and broadest intellectual and creative capacities through diverse and rigorous liberal arts learning, while also creating smart, innovative approaches to more focused career training (as noted elsewhere: primarily in public health and information technology).

Sofia's ability to courageously and lucidly critique the college project we offered ironically made her an especially strong candidate for it. Years later, she continues to pursue a career that allows her to extend and apply her creative intellect, her critical passion, and her capacity for personal independence. In the end, BPI does not dispel the questions Sofia raised, nor solve the problems that she and all our students live through every day. But it can, I hope, inform our answers to questions about the promise, and limits, of education, and what all of our institutions of higher education, public and private, selective and inclusive, can do better.

I have encountered two major surprises in doing this work. The first is how many people employed in corrections want us to be there, and to see college inside the prisons as part of a reasonable, professional approach to "corrections." Further, they are often prepared to work together in very balanced and collegial ways as the college defines its academic vision and determines curricular content. Moreover, they have been impressed and even moved by the rigorous academic discipline, intellectual breadth, and high expectations we have for our students. When creating public programs, governments often implement correctional education that looks very different from the ambitious liberal learning we do with students at Bard, or the ambitious career training one can find at the country's most innovative educational centers. But a number of correctional officials, and elected leaders, welcome what we do and take pride in it themselves.

The second major surprise, which has been less encouraging, involves the narrowed intellectual vision of many people who enter prisons to teach as philanthropic volunteers or educational activists. The faculty and administrators most prepared to embrace and engage in college in prison and to work with incarcerated students are often those most alienated from conventional pedagogy on their main campus, or most skeptical of existing standards of rigor or quality. Others drawn to teaching in prison think of it first and foremost as a form of resistance to mass incarceration or other forms of structural racism and class inequality. There is nothing wrong with such critical perspectives on existing teaching practices, or with the ambition to make our society less unequal. I share with them the belief that college in prison is one important way to expand access to American higher education. The problem is that too often academics who venture inside prison turn it into an opportunity to create something new, a chance to experiment with pedagogies or topics that are not found on the main campus.

The in-prison innovations also often mean that faculty have implemented something they consider especially progressive or radical or "relevant" to the politics of the prison space, or the imagined needs, interests, and ambitions of people in prison. When such experiments—in pedagogy or content—are consistent with what happens on their main campus on the outside, then I have no objection. But the site of prison education should not become a place markedly different from what one finds on the main campus, with either lowered academic standards, or radically altered administrative structures, or, worst of all, different ambitions for what constitutes intellectual achievement within school, or professional success after graduation.

Educational programs that engage incarcerated people in prison classrooms but fail to offer credits and degrees may be most problematic of all, especially when the work they do differs dramatically from mainstream academic practice on the conventional campus. In such well-meaning initiatives, the prison and its problems often become central to the encounter between the student and college. Such programs—lacking credits or degrees, or shorn of conventional academic standards and practices—are, typically, a lot easier to create. Such a program, associated more with social service, service learning, or "outreach," can more easily take root on the periphery of a college, since little or no institutional prestige is put at risk. Framed as an initiative not of educational achievement first and foremost, but of social justice, racial equality, or religious mission, such a project can more easily find an institutional home and grow along a path of least resistance. Deans and presidents no longer need to endorse the idea that their college "belongs" inside a prison, or that people in prison can and will be found who "belong" at such a high-achieving university. In contrast to other colleges that engage in the work—but withhold their most important forms of institutional capital—Bard was prepared to put its credits and degrees on the line from the beginning, demanding that its faculty and administration set the same expectations, standards, and ambitions for their in-prison students as they set for those on the main campus.

BPI began with the premise that the students, and the mission of the college, would be better served not by adapting to the prison, or refashioning liberal education to "intervene" in the prison, but rather by staying faithful to the college's conventional educational opportunity in all its breadth and diversity, without narrowing its scope or purpose, regardless of how well-intentioned. Faculty are recruited to represent the full breadth and diversity of what Bard already does—and as the college on the main campus evolves and changes, so too do the offerings facilitated by BPI. Thus, in contrast to the demands of a brilliant young student and woman in prison like Sofia, the Initiative was not conceived as a special intervention on behalf of a particular "population."

The commitment to hew as closely as possible to the existing (though always developing) academic requirements and structures on the main campus was made by Max and others at Bard at the outset. It was not based on a rejection of the idea that students, especially adults, can and should inform the direction of their educations. Students at BPI do just that, and often. But the college also proceeded on the assumption that its mission was to replicate the academic principles, methods, and expectations continuously developed by the college on its main, conventional campus, and to present these challenges to *all* of our students, regardless of who they are or where they study. As they mature as students, the college responds to their wishes, talents, and concerns.

Many elements of Bard's BPI curriculum are thus mandatory—the intensive first-year seminars, the grammar workshops, the "Citizen Science" training, the math literacy sequences that lead as far as the students wish to go, the need to complete a rigorous, disciplinary individualized senior thesis in order to qualify for the BA degree. Other elements of the curriculum, in contrast, have come directly from the demands made upon us by our students: German as the first foreign language, Spanish as the second, and Mandarin the third; student calls for more lab sciences, for economics, for computer programming as well as for Milton, for magic realism, for cultural studies, for diaspora and postcolonial studies and, yes, controversial or divisive subjects that obviously relate to our students' common life experiences and the challenges they and their home communities face. This approach is suffused with respect and regard for students, while rejecting the idea that college should merely prepare people to take up the existing positions that the world expects of them. This may be even more important for students from poorer and less privileged backgrounds, who, as adults, have their first genuine opportunity to study the full breadth of what the American academy has to offer.

One striking result is that after students in prison have gone to Bard for a semester or two, the demands they make on us for new topics and additional lines of coursework change and soon have little to do with the ideas that preoccupy prison activists. Our first foreign language was German because students in one of our upper-level history-anthro seminars learned of W.E.B. Du Bois's advanced studies with Max Weber in Germany. Awed by the extraordinary scope and depth of Du Bois's achievements, they demanded their own access to social theory in the original language. Later, ambitious students wanted Mandarin—which they thought had the greatest cachet in the world that lay before them after graduation and after release.

BPI's offerings in advanced mathematics, which begin where the calculus sequence ends, have similar roots in our students' preferences and achievements. Some students have on rare occasion asked for more material on the critical sociology of mass incarceration, or the social theory of punishment, and we have responded in kind. But more often, when students have the chance to pursue their own most particular interests in writing their senior projects, they do a terrific job linking their own experiences and circumstances to very broad inquiries and methods. One senior recently completed a history thesis on the role of the Roman Catholic Church in educational reform during Reconstruction. Another wrote a thesis on the successes and failures of desegregation after *Brown v. Board of Education* and other contemporary policy experiments. Another senior in the same cohort produced a thesis in abstract algebra; another on the parallels between gangsta rap and the American Western; another on European economic resilience after World War II; another on the literature of the Turkish diaspora in Berlin.

BPI has been acutely sensitive to the lowered ambitions that mark so many social programs built for the poor or institutionalized. We have largely rejected what is known as "developmental" or "remedial education"—which too often resembles the classes from which BPI's students once escaped as they fled from their failing secondary schools. Instead, we have worked hard to develop ways to combine intensive catch-up training in math and literacy with intellectual excitement and engagement of the highest order. Intellectual adventure and challenge are put first, "remediation" second, so that from day one students know that their faculty takes them seriously, and they are swept up into the cultural world and excitement of the college. They taste the thrill of the very best work before being overwhelmed by training that focuses on their deficits.

In recent years, I have advised professors and deans around the country as they have launched similar programs. All too often, the first steps taken by the most well-meaning allies are misguided. One professor at a prestigious university was frustrated by the "conservative" approach to teaching on that campus. The dean there had already rejected attempts to experiment with new pedagogies and "democratic" methods in the classroom. Frustrated, the professor thought such experiments were ideally suited for people in prison, and looked forward to doing in the prison what had not been permitted on the main campus. This strikes me now, and did then, as compromising, rather than serving, the interests of students in prison. It seemed a misuse of the prison space—regardless of whether or not the teaching "experiments" were in and of themselves a good idea. Other college administrators at prestigious schools often begin with a range of presumptions about the deficits of students they expect to meet in prison, and set out to tailor, revise, and frankly dumb down their standards and ambitions—even though driven by the best intentions.

We encourage others to resist the problematic urge to use the prison as a site of experimentation that diverges from the practices of the main campus. We urge them to resist also the well-meaning but insidious bigotry of low expectations. Whatever the flaws of existing educational practices, we think it best to avoid treating the prison as a site for enacting an idealized, albeit progressive, educational vision—out of a concern that the prison space was already subject to so many levels of "difference" and segregation that the risks were simply not worth the likely rewards. If a college that already had such pedagogies were to be transported into the prison, then the dynamics of this judgment might be moot, for students would thus be assimilated into the conventional life of the main campus.

Academically, the foundational idea was simply that students of great potential were in the prison, that the country needed to do a much better job of creating access to enriched, under-graduate education, and that it was consistent with the college's mission to do what it does best, regardless of whether it invented something new. Not because we thought the college's existing modes or vision of education were the only ones possible, or that the college wasn't a flawed institution like any other, but rather that we would betray ourselves and our students if we fashioned a special curriculum, pedagogy, or mission as the college stepped foot in the prison.

Neither BPI, nor college-in-prison of any kind, can solve the problem of mass incarceration. This deadly phenomenon, which has spread to just about every state in the country, can only be addressed by putting fewer people in prison and for less time; by making our economy less punitive; and by eliminating the stark racial disparities that mar all aspects of American inequality and especially criminal justice. Furthermore, ours is certainly not the only educational intervention possible and, considering the scale of the structural injustice represented by mass incarceration, it is hardly a panacea. But it is something that the liberal arts college, conceived as a private institution in the public interest, can do simply by playing to its existing strengths—the same way that we approach each student, not out of a primary concern for their structural oppression or their individual deficits, but instead from a love of the genius we know is within each of them. We have chosen not to reinvent ourselves based on what we thought might be appropriate to these places, or worse, "this population," but instead, in the words of Bard's president, simply to do what we do best—which is to teach. And we do this with a conviction that good—and unpredictable—things will follow.

SETTING THE TONE

One way we try to keep BPI true to the norms of Bard's campuses on "the outside" is to institute a selective admissions process. In practice, this has less to do with effectively "screening" applicants and more to do with setting the tone for how the college will address the students, regardless of their incarceration. Its significance lies primarily in how it differs not only from how many other outside or philanthropic programs address people in prison. More importantly, it represents a break with how the prison imagines and relates to people incarcerated within it who choose to become, through BPI, students first and foremost. Opening up this breach, or helping to initiative this kind of change in course, is essential to what the college can and should do. It begins well before the first day of classes.

Each summer Bard holds admissions at multiple satellite campuses in prisons across the Hudson Valley. As many people as possible who are incarcerated at a given place are notified of the opportunity and are invited to apply. Nobody is mandated to try; as many as possible, we hope, will choose to do so themselves. At Eastern, 120 people might apply to Bard out of a "general population" of about a thousand. A similar process takes place at our partner programs around the country, from Washington State to Missouri.

Applicants have to take the initiative to apply, and in doing so, they must confront a genuine risk of failure. They don't submit their high school transcripts, because most did not graduate. They don't take the SAT, and we turn a blind eye to their score on the GED, which the state requires them to pass. Instead, applicants take a timed essay exam, which is based on prompts that are short—from a single aphorism to a page or so of text—and which reflect first- and second-year college material in the humanities: poetry, political commentary, history, cultural analysis, fiction. A panel of faculty and staff then read the essays, and forty or so applicants are interviewed. In the end, fifteen students are admitted every year at any given location. At Eastern, those fifteen join an existing student body of about a hundred. Fifteen percent of the entire maximum-security prison attends Bard College full-time.

Faculty who help select students take a leap of faith with us, away from the conventional filters of private school GPAs and standardized test scores, to a relatively unmoored and discretionary process. Few if any normal filters of class, family educational history, or prior educational achievement are relevant. And while faculty are used to reading application essays, here the situation is rather different. The essay is written as a timed response to unfamiliar texts, reflective of the first-year curriculum, and written in a large room in a test-like setting. Authors will write under conditions of confinement and general surveillance, and to an audience of readers from the college who may seem particularly alien. Applicants will have had little or no preparation in how to read and write in response to the texts they are asked to read and write about. Yet beyond the long essay and the short interview that follows it for some, the admitting faculty have nothing else to go by.

Often a new professor will ask what we're looking for in the application essays. I answer that we are looking for any kind of lively response to the text—an attention to detail, an ability to treat the text as an object worthy of attention. Most broadly, we take the same approach to applicants' writing as we take to students later on: we are looking for promise, we are focusing on strengths, and, at the outset at least, marginalizing perceived weaknesses and deficits. We look for evidence of technical writing skills: composition, sentence structure, and a facility with language. I am particularly partial to syntax, thinking it's a clue to broader and deeper thinking, and a preparedness to handle and juxtapose more than one object or concept at a time. We look for flashes of voice, style, or insight. Some essays are considered strong, even though banal, if they are solidly written; others are poorly written, even borderline literate—but indicate an ability to read a sample text, to connect it meaningfully to other ideas or insights into the world beyond; or they just indicate flashes of thought that catch a faculty reader's attention. (To the general question of what to look for, I sometimes reply with an ethnic joke that, as a Jewish person, I take the liberty to share: "Two Jews are seated in a restaurant and the waiter comes over and asks: 'Hi. Is *anything* all right?'") In reading the essays, we're not there to identify shortcomings or sum up mistakes, but to search for any and all signs of strength and promise—in style, structure, clarity, creativity, or insight.

As noted in the scene that opens this book, Peter Bay's reticence at his interview was unusual. Typically, even the most anxious applicants are quite talkative and forthcoming. I have participated in many hundreds of such interviews in my fifteen years of doing this work, both in New York and across the country. In New York, we have read about 5,000 application essays (I believe I've read nearly all), and, collectively, we've interviewed probably a third of those. I recall one man who had written a brilliant essay in response to a piece of contemporary journalism on tax policy. His mother, he eventually told us, had worked at a large commercial firm in New York, and in his interview he elaborated on the incisive comments he had made in his essay about behavioral economics. (He later dual-majored in mathematics and Mandarin. Today he works as a programmer writing code.) I recall another who had noted, among many other fascinating comments, that he applied to the college because "I found myself getting comfortable in here—in prison. And this terrified me. I looked around for the best way to make myself uncomfortable again—and I chose the college." (His senior thesis, supported by extensive primary material in the original German, was on the literature of the

Turkish diaspora in Berlin. He now works at a publicity firm in Manhattan.)

The story of an applicant named John Smith indicates what can be revealed when an academic essay and personal interviews replace the standardized college admissions processes, especially those processes driven by carceral models of "correctional education." Mr Smith wore glasses and had a small reddish brown goatee and several tattoos. He was from the Appalachian region of southern Indiana along the Kentucky border, but was incarcerated in northern Indiana, in the post-industrial stretch east of Chicago and Gary. He applied to a college program based at Notre Dame, which BPI was helping to start. I was out there assisting with the first admissions process as my academic colleagues learned the ropes.

Mr Smith had dropped out of school after the tenth grade, but his admissions essay—a response to an excerpt about economic interpretations of the US Constitution—had scored among the highest in the group. He had been unanimously invited for an interview, but the conversation was going poorly. He seemed guarded and deeply suspicious. I encouraged him by saying that his essay had been quite impressive and asked him if he read a lot. No, he said, he did not.

"Well, what about writing?" I asked. "It seems you must write pretty regularly."

"No. I don't write at all," he answered stoically.

"Never a short story or a poem or a song—anything like that?"

"No."

"No letters? Surely you write letters."

"No."

"Hmm," I wondered. "What about a journal? Do you keep a journal?"

There was a short silence, then he nodded.

"I keep two journals."

"Two? Well then, so it's not essays, or letters, or what you might think of as 'college-type writing.' But it seems as if you've done a lot of writing—good writing. But did you say *two* journals?"

Another pause, and he continued. "At the end of every day in here I sit in my cell and write down what occurred on that day. Sometimes there's something in particular that I write about, what I thought about it maybe. But sometimes not. Still—every day I write down what happened in a journal, and I send it to my nine-year-old daughter."

"I see. Well, that's impressive, and that's a lot of writing. And the *second* journal?"

"I do the same thing over again—write about the day, events, things that happened. Maybe interesting, maybe not. And that one I send to my five-year-old daughter."

I can only imagine my expression when he said that.

"And you write it differently, I take it, for the younger girl?"

"Obviously."

Obvious indeed. One can hardly imagine a more revealing glimpse into the states of mind that suggest a readiness to thrive in a liberal arts college.

This admissions process speaks of how the college views itself, its future students, and its relationship to the prison. It is more than just a process to identify candidates who seem relatively ready as measured by skill, ability, or commitment. It is above all an act of *address* that begins to set the terms of the college's strange presence within the prison system—a strangeness that must be cultivated rather than minimized. The admissions process addresses the applicant about who and what we are, and, by extension, how we see them and what we expect of them. Like all modes of address, it is also an act of invocation. For the most part, it is the first time an institution of some prestige, of some significant social capital, and with an exceptionally high self-regard, has said that it sees itself, and its future, in them.

It is especially important not to exaggerate—or misinterpret—the selectivity involved in this process. Almost none of those admitted would have made it up to, let alone through, the college's "normal" screening process. (This is true at Bard, as well as at all the other selective schools, public or private, with which we now partner.) Furthermore, no matter how varied the applicant pool in any given round of admissions, we are always committed from the outset to taking a full cohort of students, and all will study on full scholarship. (Across all our campuses in New York, this amounts to about seventy new full-time college students each summer.) The same is true for the other programs we now support across the country. So the selection, which is designed to get a feel for things like relative preparedness and commitment, is balanced by the inclusiveness of always taking a full cohort.

When people observe the intellectual level of our classrooms, the high quality of student work, and the professions and graduate schools pursued by our alumni post-release, they assume that Bard is just "creaming"—selecting the relatively privileged or "middle-class" people in prison. As research shows, however, this is false. Using official state data and our own student databases, we have compared the general characteristics of BPI's entire student body—all 700 or so who have been admitted since we began—with the general prison population in New York State. It turns out that the group of people who have gotten into Bard is entirely representative of the general population in terms of ethnicity, zip code of origin, prior household income, and prior levels of educational attainment. Unfortunately, this means that students who enroll with Bard through BPI are just as poor and educationally alienated as the overwhelming majority of people in prison. Though the students go on to flourish at high levels of personal and academic achievement, they do not appear to have been filtered on the basis of preexisting social advantages. There is no "creaming." The alternative hypothesis is far more disturbing: there are untold numbers of people in prison capable of achieving at an extremely high academic level, but our existing institutions of higher education, especially those with the most financial and political capital, are overwhelmingly complacent. Those colleges and universities whose faculty, missions, and tax-exempt capital endowments put them in the privileged position to meet such students on terms of dignity and ambition are failing to do so.

In summer 2015, when the Obama administration took the remarkable step of offering Pell grants to every college and university in the United States just to experiment with offering classes to students in prison, stunningly few private colleges or universities stepped forward.

As Peter Bay expressed with such acuity during his admissions interview, prison demands that people submit to much that is imposed upon them by the institution charged with their confinement, even when their own greatest desire is to change their lives. To build a lasting college in prison is to get irredeemably tangled up in this deeply compromised process of power. But it can also help create countless opportunities for people in prison to participate in alternative "arts of the self," as they join others in building their own future and establishing an institution that reflects their own deeply personal ambitions, one that will have an impact on others who follow and whom they will never know.

Creating this self-driven, collaborative opportunity can antagonize prison staff, whose work life is often predicated upon maintaining and exerting a complex, inescapable field of control. At the very least, it can make their jobs more difficult.

Once, I sketched our desired approach while negotiating the terms of the college's admissions process with a prison official in the Midwest on behalf of one of our academic partners outside New York. As always, the sum of the technical details added up to shifting some agency toward the college, its faculty, and people in prison who wanted to join. This meant opening up new spaces in which inmates, now figured as new or prospective students, could and indeed *had* to exercise disruptive forms of agency. They would have to decide whether or not to apply, how to participate actively in the process of selection, and express themselves in the context not of the prison, exclusively, but of the college above all.

In that meeting, the prison official, who was and remains an otherwise supportive colleague, grimaced. After a short, stony silence, he said: "Well. Whatever happens, the offenders need to know that *we're* driving the bus."

People charged with the public duty of running the prison are responsible for the critical institutional decisions made within it. Hence one of the most important and delicate tasks of the college and its students is to create a common ground, whenever possible, with such officials, based on the shared interests of the people in prison, their college, and the state.

Academic selectivity in prison raises some fascinating problems, well beyond concerns over equity *within* the prison. When people in prison choose to apply for college, they are actively looking for ways to distinguish themselves and change their lives. For a conventional prestigious college, this is all good. Selective schools understand themselves and their students in precisely such terms. This selectivity is bound up with the college's worldly status and informs its institutional culture—the daily practices of how students, faculty, and administrators relate to each other and constitute their relationships.

But in the eyes of many experts who view the matter through the lenses of criminal justice policy or social science methodology, this is a problem. The people who distinguish themselves with initiative and promise are, from an academic perspective, meeting the college on familiar terms and participating in its values of autonomy and ambition. But from the perspective of those whose aim is to prove what "works" to reduce recidivism, this "self-selection" ruins the social science. Their concern is generating evidence to justify college in prison by showing that it has the "effect" of "reducing recidivism" and hence can lower crime and save money. Indeed, such thinking goes, "If people choose to do this, then surely they were already the ones who weren't coming back?" The search to prove a causal relationship between the independent variable (college) and the dependent variable (recidivism) has been polluted by an admissions process based on desire, initiative, and freedom—the lifeblood of a genuine education.

The expert's preoccupation with "dosage" signals an overwhelming concern with how many units of college it takes to lower recidivism by margins that justify the cost. The logical implication is that we are compelled to avoid the disastrous outcome of an "overdose" of education (especially, no doubt, an overdose of the liberal arts). One might sympathize with the lawyer and social theorist Otto Kirscheimer, who once quipped that "all public policy is irrational, but none is as irrational as criminal justice policy." But even if one is less pessimistic than this, it is clear that the criminal justice paradigm, preoccupied as it is with lowered recidivism and a search for the efficient "dosage" of education, parts ways not only with faculty and students, but with the spirit of liberal learning and higher education itself.

Supporters of this work must recognize that the college's potential in prison can only be fully realized through a cumbersome, sometimes tense, and often arm's-length collaboration, in which the college and prison keep a respectful distance from each other and focus on cultivating a common ground between them while recognizing their essential distinctiveness. If the partnership becomes too close, and the institutions become indistinguishable from each other, the opportunity is squandered. This separation, and the respectfully managed tension that results, is a good thing, is indeed an essential thing. Its loss, the excessive meshing of gears or even merger between a college and a prison, indicates most clearly where education ends and another branch of corrections begins.

A student like Peter or Sofia in New York or John Smith in Indiana gets a letter through the prison mail. They come to orientation and go on to take classes most of every day, most days of the week, for most of every year. Ideally, something like this goes on as long as possible until they go home from prison. The basic questions are easy: can they get along in class, adjust to the norms of the college, and master the skills that faculty demands in order to get a degree? Peter Bay was going to encounter many people and texts that would challenge his beliefs and unsettle his habits of thought and speech. He would find himself in new kinds of confrontations, and new alliances, with different kinds of authorities.

This would be Bay's daily life in the college, shared with more than a hundred other men in the prison who had chosen a similar path. They realize that the work of the college is hard, and forces them, continually and rather publicly, to confront their own shortcomings and limitations. Each day they will move in and out of the college and back through the surrounding institutional spaces where the prison regime holds sway. Their daily movement takes them between the prison spaces and the college's makeshift campus, which emerges fluidly, whenever its students gather, with or without faculty, and sets in motion their distinct structures of authority, discourse, and affiliation.

Almost without exception, graduates of Bard's Prison Initiative leave prison and never come back. For all of the personal achievement their academic careers embody, the only fact most people will care about is the one that interests their college the least: that after fifteen years the recidivism rate for all participants is about 4 percent and for graduates around 2 percent. Once they go home, many students disappear from the college's view. The only trace we have of them is their absence from state criminal justice records. However, many other alumni remain in touch, often becoming members of an active community, finishing Bard or other undergraduate degrees after release, going on to professions and careers, mentoring others who follow them into careers in social services, opening doors to jobs at private companies where they themselves are employed, or helping them prepare for graduate school in scholarly fields or the professions.

BPI alumni have gone on to study at more than thirty-five schools, both public and private, ranging from community colleges to leading centers of international research. Among these alumni, several have completed or are completing graduate degrees in epidemiology from Columbia; others who have master's or even PhDs across the CUNY system and in social work from Hunter, urban planning and sociology from NYU, or divinity from Yale. They have developed plays at the Public Theater and scholarly articles on education and ethics; they are computer programmers and successful small-business owners. Some are laying sheet metal, others are executives at for-profit firms, or rising stars in organizations devoted to social service or legal reform. Some are becoming mathematicians and others electricians. This very diversity of careers is a testament to the inclusiveness, and the excellence, of the opportunity they have encountered.

IN FACT, LIBERAL learning is not in crisis. The contents and methods of the liberal arts will continue to appeal to some people, but hardly all, and in any case will be accessible to far too few. The meaning of the liberal arts will evolve, as it has for centuries, as will the technologies and social relations that determine how it is pursued and by whom. Prevailing inequalities will continue to disfigure the labor—and leisure—that constitutes a life of learning, and economies of distinction will continue to inform the definition of education and the values ascribed to it. For all of this, the liberal arts will continue to be meaningful and even essential elements of human emancipation.

Our pressing problem lies not in the vision or definition of the liberal arts, and certainly not in the technologies that will continue to alter its practice. But we do have significant problems in the institutions of higher learning charged with carrying this tradition forward on terms that are appropriate for a democratic society. Entrusted with a function that is at once so personal and so public, our best institutions are not doing enough to transcend the increasingly privileged worlds in which they operate. The perceived crisis in the academy is not about the poverty or ossification of our traditions but about our institutional failure to take the risks needed to find students in unconventional places and engage them at critical moments in their lives.

CHAPTER 2

Landscapes

BPI AND MASS INCARCERATION

RACE IS A fallacy with great power, permanently woven into the fabric of American life. To engage it, in the words of James Baldwin writing in "Many Thousands Gone," is "to become involved with the force of life and legend . . . creating that dense, many-sided and shifting reality which is the world we live in and the world we make."

In prison in the United States, any college that takes up this work involves itself with an institution that plays a leading role in producing racial inequality. Furthermore, a "culture of control" as well as a life of punitive economic insecurity has characterized the political economy of the United States and other similarly situated countries in the past forty years. Among more and more people of all subject positions, especially the working classes, this culture of control embraces and reaches beyond racial prejudice and structural racism, as a wide array of Americans face growing levels of surveillance, punitiveness, and insecurity in ever more facets of our daily lives. As a college in prison, BPI is deeply inflected by race and racial inequality. By extension, of course, I as a white middle-class male exist in the world as a racial subject, and this informs and affects my experience and perception of the work at perhaps all levels. At the same time, I think it would be a mistake to subsume BPI's importance (or my roles within it) entirely under that heading, just as it is probably a mistake to analyze mass incarceration exclusively as an engine for reproducing racial inequality.

As an institution dedicated to the practice of liberal-arts learning, BPI must inevitably engage with the complex reality of racial inequality, precisely in order to fulfill the breadth and integrity of its intellectual and democratic purpose. Analysing the experience and production of race, inequality, and our myriad ways of being and acting in the world constitutes much of what is done across a host of disciplines and practices in liberal learning. While engaging with these central features of the college, BPI must also chart a course that embraces the full variety and vitality of intellectual, analytic, and creative activity. Such issues inform and shape my own ways of acting across infinite moments of teaching, advising, and institution-building. They also pose particular challenges, I think, to someone who assumes a position in between college in prison, its students, and broader constituencies. They therefore play an important part in how I take stock of my successes or failures over the years, as I have tried to keep faith with the traditions of liberal learning and earn the respect of the students with whom I have worked.

A starkly disproportionate number of people in prison are African American. Many are also white, Asian, and Latino. Indeed, in most states across the country, African Americans are not the majority of people in prison, meaning that while mass incarceration is a phenomenon rooted in racial modes of inequality, over-incarceration is *also* an inclusive phenomenon touching all Americans, especially poor Americans of every racial and ethnic background. The African American experience of economic inequality is acutely disproportionate and uniquely intense, while the effects of criminal law, policing regimes, and punitive criminal justice, perhaps always but especially since the 1970s, pervades the lives of all but the most privileged Americans, and the culture of control likely constitutes and disfigures the lives of even its most privileged classes.

BPI's place in relation to the racialized field of the prisons within which it works is especially complicated. As a liberal arts college, part of its mission is training students to engage in a thoughtful critique of their own lives and society. Confronting the racialized nature of American inequality, and of the prison especially, is thus not only inevitable; it is an essential part of the education. For this and related reasons, the liberal arts have a unique role to play inside the prison. Further, over time, our academic institutions are themselves both pushed and pulled to engage with their own historical and present-day roles in the reproduction of racial and other inequalities. And finally, a liberal education also includes what I might call a broader constellation of educational ambitions that embrace these specific egalitarian or emancipatory projects, but often go beyond them as well.

BPI's student body is disproportionately African American, reflecting the racial inequality that defines New York's criminal justice system. And yet at many of BPI's campuses in New York and across the consortium of partner programs we have helped create, most people in prison are of other ethnic or racialized identities, and this too is reflected in the student body of different college-in-prison programs. As discussed in the previous chapter, BPI replicates the education offered on its main campus inside prisons, allowing the prison as a field to shape the academic architecture only in minimal ways, or perhaps more accurately, in ways that are already characteristic of the education on the main campus. Students enrolled with BPI have ample opportunity to engage with diverse and complex aspects of race and inequality across their studies. Often they initiate such studies themselves, and just as often such inquiries are woven into the course materials, syllabi, and academic training of faculty. Moreover, these themes are not made distinctive features of the curriculum because it is developed in the highly racialized and class-sensitive space of the prison. Instead, they appear and are incorporated as inherent elements of study that should and often do characterize the contemporary liberal arts campus.

This chapter will reflect on some of the complexities that give BPI its peculiar character, specifically in relation to the racialized nature of mass incarceration. The vehicle for this reflection is the story of a Bard class I taught for BPI in the early 2000s on American legal history. The material and topics of this course reflected my training in history, literature, and law, and my own place on the Bard faculty as a lecturer in law and the humanities. The bulk of the material explored antebellum U.S. legal history with a focus on the political and legal relationship between the Constitution and slavery. The origin of this course lay far from the prison—I taught it originally at the Rhetoric Department at the University of California at Berkeley, and later on Bard's main campus. For me, teaching it for BPI reflected both a continuity of educational vision and, inevitably, a departure as well. Some of my classes have been on topics like liberalism in the American political tradition or "constitutional discourse." This one, however, was one of the classes I have taught for BPI that have diverged from the Bard and BPI norm in that it implicated the prison in general and mass incarceration in particular. For that reason I have chosen this course as a vehicle to explore some of the resonance between the liberal arts college understood most broadly, and the context in which BPI operates inside contemporary American prisons.

ORIENTATION

In 2002, Max and I started expanding BPI beyond its Eastern campus by opening a pilot program at Greene Correctional Facility, about thirty minutes north of Bard. Greene was a medium-security prison with a large proportion of younger inmates and others with shorter sentences. Typically, the security level of a prison indicates the proximity of its inmates to release, rather than reflecting the underlying nature of their conviction. Like many medium-security prisons, therefore, Greene was a more transient and volatile environment than Eastern. It's not uncommon to find that maximum-security prisons like Eastern offer a better environment for the sort of long-term, stable relationships between a college and a student that BPI fosters.

The relationship between the college and Eastern had been forged directly between Max and the superintendent and senior staff. The private capital he organized within the void of public funding gave us the liberty to design and implement things in keeping with the college's own academic vision and institutional culture. At Greene things were different. We were there because parties in New York City and Washington had compelled some leaders of the state Department of Corrections in Albany to direct some of its federal funding away from exclusively vocational programs to include a subcontract with a liberal arts college.

Our college pilot at Greene was to operate with public, federal funds, controlled on the ground, like all "block grants," by state officials. Most importantly, the age group eligible for these federal funds was only to run between 18 and 24, which would yield a significantly younger median age for the students than we had become used to at Eastern. Furthermore, it appeared that the system's leadership was divided over the need for college in prison, and it was also working under a broad political division over the idea of higher education for incarcerated people. As a result of negotiations elsewhere, the pilot at Greene was not to culminate in a degree, but in a "post-secondary" certificate considered less controversial, and perhaps more appropriate, than an actual college degree. It was to focus exclusively on people as close to release as possible, and thus would be at a "medium"-security facility like Greene, rather than a longer-term one like Eastern. Overall, then, the program at Greene had a broader policy profile, but the autonomy of the college had been reduced, and the dynamics of the classroom potentially altered by who was eligible to participate, and how.

In marked contrast to the approach we had been developing at Eastern, the DOC selected the participants for that year at Greene using standardized tests, educational diagnostics, and by identifying whomever they could who fit the narrow requirements imposed on the experiment by federal authorities. There was no college admissions process of the kind we had carefully replicated at Eastern. The ethos of corrections thus shaped the program at Greene from the outset far more than it had at Eastern. The processes at Eastern by which people in prison took the initiative to apply, write an essay, and interview in response to an open invitation from the college had been more or less eliminated. The students, I was to discover, were often there halfheartedly, and I never quite understood what mixture of positive incentive and negative compulsion had been used to get them there.

Now the first thing to follow every BPI process was a group orientation between all of the new students and two representatives of the college, who in those early days were Max and myself. These orientations have always been, and should remain, charged personal events. The nerve-wracking process of admissions is passed, and the formation of a new cohort of colleagues, and future friends, begins in earnest. The orientations follow a familiar ceremonial pattern: we acknowledge the risk that they all have taken to apply, confronting unique personal and institutional obstacles, and thank them for having trusted us enough to assume that the college would make it worthwhile, after which we congratulate them on getting in. We typically followed with brief introductions of ourselves, our roles at Bard, and a remark or two about what first drew us to this work: in my case, I would always discuss with a bit of irony the privilege I had of growing up in a household that cultivated both a lifelong love of learning as well as a fairly deep distrust and even dislike of institutions, especially schools. This was always followed by a statement about how the college sees the setting up of mini-campuses inside, and the search for terrific students who happen to be incarcerated, as part of a far larger commitment to the significance and power of the liberal arts, and the benefit of establishing it in places—often in other parts of the world—where liberal arts learning has been absent, or actively excluded.

Students were then invited to introduce themselves to us and to each other, and to state, if possible, what had brought them to apply to the college. One of the most memorable over the years was from a student who said he'd been in prison for several years and had recently found himself "getting comfortable." This, he said, shocked and disturbed him. "So I looked around for a way to make myself *uncomfortable* again in here," he said, smiling, "and the college was the obvious choice." An informal group chat ends with a satisfying ritual of students' filling out the college matriculation forms, and then turn toward a discussion of the launch of classes, the first year's curriculum, and a review of the college's basic academic policies.

At all of our previous orientations, these gatherings were suffused with high spirits, the excitement of new beginnings, and the students' manifest pleasure at having gotten in. At a deeper and more tacit level, there is the excitement of gathering, with strangers, to undertake something ambitious and unknown, together. Before Greene, the mood had always been profoundly shaped by the various students' own individual decisions to apply, and efforts to get in. The result was a grouping that was unusual, if not unique, inside the prison—for most of the new students are strangers to each other before the orientation, and represent, proportionally, nearly every age, ethnic group, and religious affiliation inside the prison. Largely regardless of who they were, and most of their other political and religious views, they shared the fact that they had decided for themselves that the college was the place they wanted to be. Crucial meaning and energy comes from the fact that the program is not mandated by the courts, incentivized by sentencing law, or initiated by the prisons, and that the group as a whole is made up of students who have chosen to join, but *not* on the basis of their pre-existing religious, ethnic, or political affiliations. Their diversity of life-histories, ambitions, and uncertainties, and the agency they've exercised to get into that room, all resonate quite deeply with the spirit and practice of the liberal arts that will form the content and structure of the studies that lie ahead. At Greene, of course, the magic of the orientation had been complicated, and compromised, by the selection process, which had remained in the realm of corrections, rather than being rooted in the distinct dynamics of the college inside.

As was our habit from the several orientations we had done in the preceding years at Eastern, our introduction of the program involved a short discussion of the history of college in prison in New York. In particular, we discussed the vulnerability of such programs, and the controversy that had come to surround them as the political upheavals around crime had reached a peak in the late 1980s and early 1990s. These culminated in the revocation of Pell eligibility as part of the enormously complex and hotly debated Omnibus Crime Bill of 1994.

When we had raised these issues previously at the maximum-security Eastern orientations, the conversations had gone much differently. Older, often incarcerated longer, many of the students there experienced first-hand the destruction of college-in-prison programs in the 1990s. Lively discussions followed; older students explained the history to the younger ones in the room, and spoke of their personal experiences as students back in the days of Pell, and the anger and heartbreak that followed their collapse. But at Greene, the younger students had no personal experience of this history, and seemed to have heard nothing about it.

Sitting in the circle at Greene, I told the story of New York's "last graduation"—the final graduation of a college in prison in New York that had been held in 1994, just after the passage of the Crime Bill. I based my account on a documentary film by Barbara Zahn, *The Last Graduaton*, which had recounted the political origins of college-in-prison in New York and the successes of students. It had vividly depicted how central it had felt to them as they repaired their lives and the lives of their families, and the heartbreak they had felt when the programs were abruptly dismantled. The students at Greene that day said nothing in response to this narrative, and sat silently, in contrast to the way the topic had brought students together at Eastern and honed their sense of the preciousness—and vulnerability—of what they were about to begin.

Several days later, Max was asked about our orientation by state officials, who had heard from local staff at the prison alarmed that we'd gathered the students together as a group, outside of class and before the semester had officially begun. They were obviously still getting used to the new dynamics the college established, and the somewhat unusual and seemingly informal ways that college staff would be relating with students. Such practices had become familiar at Eastern, where they were part of the normal functioning of "the program," but were novel at Greene. Perhaps the negotiations that had been required to even make this unusual, publicly funded experiment happen at all had also put everyone on edge. As Max answered candidly about the nature of our orientation, officials expressed their discomfort. They didn't mind the new mode of collegiality, it seemed, so much as our decision to emphasize the history of college-in-prison in New York, and the controversial nature of its eradication a decade earlier. Above all, they felt we had been divisive, setting the college up in opposition to our partners in corrections in the eyes of the students.

Now when Congress had debated the revocation of Pell eligibility in the 1990s, the nation's wardens were among the most vocal in testifying *on behalf* of college-in-prison programs. They argued that these programs were among the best interventions going on inside, and entirely consummate with their larger mission of corrections. Yet at the time, it's true, I was inclined to dwell on the differences between the private college and our partners in state government. These differences were real and at times profound. There was, it's true, a longstanding tradition of departments working with private and public colleges and universities to offer opportunity to people in prison, in New York and nationwide. Yet in 1994, the professional civil servants had been overruled by the politicians, and the politics of funding such programs remained divisive. The passions around that conflict were still quite heightened when we started at Greene. The officials were animated, antagonized, and for a moment Max thought the experiment at Greene might end before it had truly begun, but in the end, they let us off with a reprimand and the project continued as planned.

In hindsight, the depth of my discussion about the politics of Pell revocation, and its impact within the prisons in the immediate area, may have put our partners in the department in a difficult position. And it's true that my telling might have easily been read as divisive. Additionally, it may have placed the students in a difficult situation. Had I expected them to respond frankly to us, young Bard staff and total strangers whose relationship to them must have seemed ambiguous? After all, the topic was not only how important and meaningful college in prison had been in recent American history, but also how the shift in federal policy had removed funding from the prisons in which they themselves were incarcerated. It was not a bad idea to discuss at the outset that there was something particularly sensitive—and perhaps inspiring—about the project we were starting together. But I had failed to appreciate the sensitivity of the students' position in charting their relationship to the sort of college opportunity that, so recently, had been built up so successfully only to then be taken away.

Geography of Punishment

Since launching the project at Greene, BPI's network has come to include six satellite campuses inside prisons across the Hudson Valley, five for men and one for women. Crucially, the five Bard campuses for men are interconnected: people in prison enroll with the college at a higher-level maximum-security prison farther upstate. As their security level drops over time, they can move to another prison, closer to the city downstate, where Bard also has a satellite campus, thus remaining continuously enrolled and closely involved with their college for long, intensive periods of study up to and through release.

BPI can be understood, then, as intervention in what I refer to as the "geography of punishment." This thinking is informed by, but is somewhat different from, the work done on mass incarceration by academics in the field of political geography. Roughly speaking, it is my impression that in New York the more severe a person's sentence, and the earlier he or she is during a term of incarceration, the farther they are removed from New York City, held in regions along the Canadian border or in the deep west upstate. The remoteness of these places from home, the poverty of resources nearby, and the social distance between inmates and staff all serve to intensify the punitiveness of the experience. However, as prisoners' time to release draws nearer, they become eligible to move down from the most remote prisons to facilities closer to New York City. During a sentence, people in prison may be rewarded by movements downstate, and punished by renewed exile farther away, one of the infinite dynamics of "incentive," reward, and punishment that help define the character of the system itself. Over time, incremental transfers to prisons farther south can bring the incarcerated person closer to family members who long to visit, and to forms of metropolitan social capital that can make its way into the prison system: church groups, lawyers, public health practitioners, and the like.

It is not uncommon for people in a New York prison to work within the system of counselors and managers, doing what they can to be moved to a site where Bard has a campus. This becomes an element of the agency that people in prison exercise in relation to the larger system that BPI tries to enhance. It is amplified many times over, as the student and the college develop intermediary relationships shaped by, but quite distinct from, the context of the prison and its overarching system of control. For those enrolled, the space and time of the prison is partially transformed into the space and time of the college. The length, continuity, and purposiveness of the relationship between student and college are unlike nearly any other institutional relationship within the prison landscape. (One Bard BA senior thesis in anthropology, written by a student then in prison, is an ethnographic exploration of the effects of college enrollment on the experience of prison space and time; that student is now a vice president at an industrial company in New York City.) The resulting collegiate relationship can and must, stand between the prison and those in its custody every day. Thus by "geography of punishment" I refer to how incarcerated people are moved through space *within* the prison system and how BPI has developed a structure of satellite campuses in ways that redefine the system's dislocations.

The dynamic between Bard, its students, and the administrative patterns of correctional population movement plays out within much larger patterns of population management shaped by relations of race and class. An extensive scholarship focuses on this political geography of mass incarceration. Notable work includes Ruth Wilson Gilmore's groundbreaking study of the growth of prisons in California and work by Peter Wagner and others on the unequal impact of geographically targeted sentencing laws (like "safe school zones") and, even more notoriously, the gerrymandering effects of felon disenfranchisement.

Highly detailed graphic information systems, called "Justice Mapping" and pioneered by Eric Cadora (for whom I worked in New York City before coming to BPI), use advanced techniques to visually represent the flows of population and public money created by our patterns of arrest and incarceration. This mapping was first developed extensively in New York, just about the time BPI was being launched. With access to sensitive state and city policing data, Cadora generated finely grained maps that tracked block by block every arrest in New York City that led to incarceration upstate. This data was then merged with records of criminal justice *spending*, including the per-capita annual cost of incarceration. As curated by Laura Kurgan and the Spatial Information and Design Labs at Columbia University, the resulting maps tracked the migratory flow of persons, and money, created by existing criminal justice policies, dollar by dollar, body by body. The resulting picture reveals how huge sums of criminal justice spending are triggered in the poorest urban neighborhoods, where crime and victimization are highest, but are then spent hundreds of miles away—in other poor communities—where prisons are located. The concentration of criminal justice initiated in poor urban neighborhoods, but spent outside of them, "is," in the words of Jennifer Gonnerman, "so dense that states are spending in excess of a million dollars a year to incarcerate the residents of single city blocks." In Brooklyn, there have been as many as thirty-five "million-dollar blocks"—though all of this money is spent not on local interventions, but on prisons hundreds of miles away. For some of the poorest blocks, the price tag of this criminal justice population movement has surpassed five million dollars per year per block.

This extreme imbalance between where crime and victimization occur—in densely populated poor neighborhoods—and the money that is spent far away on incarceration is among the most telling features of our current approach to crime. The majority of New York's prisons lie "upstate"—in rural and ex-urban areas that have suffered terribly from the decline of family-owned agriculture and domestic manufacturing since the 1970s. In these regions jobs and young people have been leaving for decades. Governor Nelson Rockefeller, in partnership with the state legislature, built dozens of new prisons. In 1970, New York had twenty prisons. By 1990 it had seventy. This is the generation in which American total incarceration went from 300,000 to over 2.5 million. This sort of prison infrastructure, as famously charted by Eric Schlosser and analyzed in greater depth by Gilmore and others, was thus built on a social foundation that is very hard to change. Increasingly isolated and overwhelmingly white communities upstate became dependent on public-sector jobs devoted to the incarceration of disproportionately poor people of color from downstate and other urban areas. The ethnic and class divisions of the state's political geography were thus cemented into the state's prison infrastructure.

The monetary dynamics of prison geography in turn led to perverse dynamics in the funding of college in prison. In New York, the community college system has long been funded in part through an accounting formula known as the "charge-back" system. Campuses in counties all across the state are reimbursed by, or "charge back," the state for each student enrolled. But in this system, not all students are created equal. Instead, a student from a downstate metropolitan area generates a substantially higher reimbursement to a community college than a student who comes from a rural county upstate. The idea, I suppose, was that metropolitan community colleges would have a higher overhead, and so warranted a higher revenue flow from the state treasury. But for some reason, the designers of this system built it so that the increased funding followed the students, based on their home zip codes, rather than simply paying downstate campuses more based on enrollments on site. So if an upstate community college campus enrolled a student from downstate, it generated significantly more revenue in "charge backs" than if it had simply filled the same seat with a local student from its own surrounding area.

When this charge-back system—creating different money values for students from different neighborhoods—merged with the population movements driven by mass incarceration, the effects were insidious. In the 1980s and 1990s, when state and federal tuition funding was still available for people in prison, upstate community colleges had a strong incentive to set up programs inside the local state prison—where nearly all of the potential students would have come from homes downstate (in or near one of those million-dollar blocks). In the public reimbursement or "charge-back" economy, incarcerated students were a far richer source of revenue for a local upstate community college than young people from the school's own region. Some community colleges lived on the differentials, floating the conventional campus on the revenues generated by enrolling in-prison students. When the public funding for college in prison disappeared, some community campuses were threatened with shutting down entirely, as they no longer enjoyed the extra revenue generated from incarcerated students who had been brought upstate by the coercive movement of population that the prison system generated.

MASS INCARCERATION AND THE
REPRODUCTION OF RACIAL CASTE

These micro and macro dynamics of spending on college and prison fit into a larger phenomenon, of course: the advent, since the 1970s, of mass incarceration in the United States. The term "mass incarceration," as used by the sociologist Bruce Western and many others, refers not merely to the historically unprecedented rate of incarceration that marks American society as a whole, but, much more specifically, to the hyper-incarceration imposed on African Americans. While about 15 percent of New York State's population is African American, around 50 percent of its prison population is (and this is true of BPI's New York–based student community). These are young adults from poor, urban areas; or older men, often with a son, father, or grandson in the system as well. They grew up in neighborhoods with the highest numbers of crimes but also of victims, which it is too easy for others to forget. Perpetrators and victims are overwhelmingly from the same communities, contrary to the racialized and classist distortions in the popular white imagination. African Americans make up roughly 13 percent of the U.S. population, but account for almost 40 percent of its prisoners. Even when one brackets their preexisting and disproportionate rates of poverty (a condition that correlates with, but is also reinforced by, imprisonment and its structural, collateral effects), a racial subject-position still reveals a threefold disparity. That is, poor black people are six times more likely to go to prison than all Americans, and all black people regardless of economic class are three times more likely to go prison than poor white people.

These facts are uncontested; but the analysis of their causes and significance is a subject of some debate. The civil rights lawyer and policy advocate Michele Alexander has popularized the idea that the mass incarceration is the result of a host of failed economic and criminal justice policies, including a backlash against civil rights. In her highly influential *The New Jim Crow: Mass Incarceration in the Era of Color-Blindness*, Alexander summarizes an extensive literature that shows how laws that appear racially neutral, above all in the criminalization of drug policy, have had a highly disproportionate and massively harmful impact on African Americans. In the analysis of public policy and its effects, she wishes—quite rightly—to shift the discussion from a narrow, individualistic concern with "discriminatory intent," in which conscious racism is the problem, to a social and structural focus on "disparate impact," in which real-world outcomes that disproportionately affect minorities are recognized as suspect and as major problems for law and social policy.

I, among others, share many of Alexander's views. But I also find convincing the arguments proposed by scholars such as James Forman Jr. and Marie Gottschalk, who appear to endorse many of the most important fundamentals of Alexander's "Jim Crow" framework while offering some compelling critiques as well. Most importantly, perhaps, Forman argues that Alexander's approach can have the effect of minimizing the historical Jim Crow by obscuring the ferocity of its extreme physical violence and systematic racial terror. In a larger context in which reparations remain a vital political conversation, this is a matter of both historical vision and, potentially, practical political import.

Part of the problem in developing a nuanced analysis of mass incarceration lies in the tendency of some advocates, including Alexander, to emphasize the importance of the "war on drugs" and the numbers of people in prison for nonviolent offenses. This is, undoubtedly, a huge problem. But in truth, the larger problem of structural racism includes not only the disastrously disproportionate criminalization of the drug trade and addiction since the 1980s, but also the epidemic of violence and violent victimization within poor and African American communities as well. Unfortunately, the Jim Crow narrative often obscures the fact that the majority of people in prison are actually serving sentences for violent crimes. This is *not* to say that mass incarceration is not a disaster, and one of the most important forms of racialized inequality: it is. But this adjusted view does make the landscape of contemporary criminal justice practices more complicated than that of the apartheid system of historical Jim Crow, while suggesting that the contemporary problem of mass incarceration is more nuanced and, perhaps, more difficult to tackle than simply rolling back things like mandatory sentencing regimes and abandoning the grievous and racialized approach to the criminalization of drugs. Advocates tend to ignore or occlude the significant numbers of people in prison for violent crime, and to focus most if not all of their polemic on the criminalization of drugs; this is a problem. The complexity of African American leadership's positions on drugs and crime in the 1970s and 1980s, as hotly debated by the historians Donna Murch and Jessica Neptune and by the political scientist Michael Javen Fortner, complicates the picture even more. But the fact remains that were the United States to release from prison *everyone* convicted of nonviolent drug crimes, the remaining prison population would *still* amount to an all-time high in the rate of American incarceration. In the eyes of many of America's leading scholars and social scientists, the criminal justice system, with its pervasive class inequalities and racially disparate impacts, has become, in the words of Murch, "the biggest obstacle to black equality since legalized segregation."

In *The Prison and the Gallows: The Politics of Mass Incarceration in America*, and most recently in *Caught*, the political scientist Marie Gottschalk offers the best comprehensive account of the wide-ranging scholarly literature aimed at understanding mass incarceration, including its racial injustice. *Caught* provides a full synopsis of the work done to understand mass incarceration, in ways that include but also complicate the Jim Crow narrative. In part, Gottschalk engages the work of scholars as diverse as David Garland and Loïc Wacquant, who situate the emergence of mass incarceration within the context of even broader changes in social policy and the welfare state associated with major shifts in the state and economy that intensified in the early 1970s. Alexander's racial analysis of American criminal justice policy has helped launch the issue into the foreground of the national awareness. Yet Gottschalk may be quite right to remind us that "a movement to challenge the carceral state centered on black-white disparities in the criminal justice system ignores how the carceral state" affects "immigrants, poor whites, and people charged with sex offenses," and that it comes at a high political cost, marginalizing other "key inequalities associated with the seepage of neoliberalism into all aspects of public policy."

In the words of Craig Wilder, a historian who is deeply familiar with these questions as both a scholar and a teacher: "The anti-black underpinnings of American institutions and the disproportionately negative consequences of recent criminal justice policies on African American communities invite, and, at times, necessitate, placing black people at the center of the mass incarceration critique. However, decentering race from this debate has benefits." I believe that Alexander, and others devoted to leading the country on a very different course, would defend the absolute importance of the racial analysis *and* embrace an inclusive strategy for both social analysis and political change, as Gottschalk has advocated.

The scholarly literature around mass incarceration is diverse, contested, and growing—as it should and must be. But as far as college in prison is concerned, it is important to step back and insist on a heavy dose of modesty when assessing what impact the work of BPI and others has had in providing access to higher education for those who are caught up in this system. Regardless of how we analyze the problem of mass incarceration and strategize about dismantling it, neither the Bard Prison Initiative nor any college-in-prison program can offer a structural solution to mass incarceration. This is important to remember because, as Ellen Lagemann has argued, American liberalism is always tempted to dream that education can do too much, forcing it to become what Saul Bellow called "the great recompense." The sort of intensive, rigorous, long-term education that is at the heart of BPI's work is unlikely to engage the preponderance of those who are incarcerated. Even as we succeed in bringing far more public and private educational institutions into the work, as may occur in the years ahead, this serves to address, but not solve, the underlying problems of unequal access to American higher education and the more crushing but related inequalities perpetuated by criminal justice policy. College in prison is a way to improve the quality and mission of American higher education and to address the humanity of incarcerated people, creating islands of relative health, opportunity, and growth. But the problem of mass incarceration can only begin to be addressed through fundamentally different approaches to sentencing and radically altered views of the justification and purposes of punishment. This point is driven home by a range of excellent scholars and practitioners from Marc Mauer at the Sentencing Project in Washington, DC, to James Austin and, among others, Michael Jacobson at the CUNY Institute for State and Local Governance.

There is every reason, both principled and practical, to reduce both the scale and the brutal indignity of incarceration. Beyond this, we need fundamental correction of the inequalities in all areas of our lives, including criminal justice, education, and employment. BPI, with its commitment to liberal learning, the dignity of students, and a bit of institutional activism, is an important piece of what is and should be a much broader conversation about access and opportunity within American higher education.

At the level of curriculum, pedagogy, and academic structure, BPI has, I think, tried to chart an intelligent course forward, just as others are showing us ways to navigate the politics of mass incarceration as leaders and engaged scholars. BPI seeks to remain true to both the profound realities of the racialized nature of the prisons within which our students begin their higher education, and to the broadest mission and values of liberal learning, so that the diverse aspects of the work reinforce each other. While inevitably limited in scope and scale, BPI and many similar programs can offer a small but important part of what can be, in the words of the MIT historian and regular BPI faculty member Craig Wilder, "a way out of the failed policies of mass incarceration—if we have the courage to take it."

LLOYD ADAMS

This, then, was the larger landscape within which we began BPI's experimental expansion at Greene Correctional Facility. After our awkward overture to the students and the reprimand that followed, we resumed our work, perhaps with a keener understanding of the tensions between prison staff, the college, and our new student at Greene. When I first went in to Greene to teach I was joined by Justus Rosenberg, an emeritus professor from Bard who, just past his seventieth birthday, had volunteered at once to teach for BPI. Like many of the central figures at Bard College, Justus had been a refugee. He was born in Leipzig, a free city-state in Germany. When the Nazis were about to invade, his parents, whom he never saw again, sent him off to France, where he survived a proto-concentration camp, escaped, and joined the French Resistance. Later, he completed a doctorate at the Sorbonne before making his way to the United States.

Justus and I were picked up by a DOCCS minivan and driven across the barren tarmac to the barracks designated for school. During the slow drive, Justus spoke freely in his eloquent, gregarious manner about his class—an introduction to "genres" of world literature (he pronounced "genres" in French with a flourish). He brought me up to date on the progress of the *memoir* he was writing. When he first came to Bard College in the 1960s, he represented the entire department of foreign languages and literature. Back then, when Bard was tiny, if you wanted to study French, you went to Justus; if you wanted Italian, German, or Russian, you went to Justus: he was fluent in the languages and cultures of them all.

Processed and cleared by guards behind desks and thick glass, official visitors pass through an electrically bolted sally port and are released into the prison grounds. The compound was silent, and groups of young black men in green uniforms were being marched across the grounds from a distance. We were unexpectedly dropped off at the infirmary and told we were to have our TB test before the first day's classes began. Justus fell silent as the nurse rolled up the sleeve on his worn but flawlessly tailored silk shirt, with its frayed Eton collar, revealing the numbers tatooed on his arm. The two-minute van ride back across the bleak prison grounds, barracks, and trailers seemed interminable, and I was grateful to Justus for the return of his indomitable energy, wit, and cheer. His monologue wove back and forth between a report on the two medals he had won swimming in the Senior Olympics, and the delight he was taking in teaching the stories of Colette and Mahasweta Devi this semester, both on the main campus and here at Greene. We passed a small area about 100 feet in diameter, near the center of the prison compound, halfway between the fortified entrance and the mute facade of the school building. This odd, central patch of empty ground was surrounded by its own elaborate chain link fence and razor wire. Inside was nothing but some grass, and what appeared to be a natural pond, with cattails and green tall grasses growing up around it. The prison, after intense legal wrangling, had been built in the middle of a federally protected wetland, and this peculiar patch of "protected" land in the middle of the prison was part of the regulators' compromise. Justus and I watched as a heron made its way over the razor wire, at a steep ascent, and flew off toward the Catskills.

The syllabus of my course that semester at Greene ran from the framing of the Constitution to the outbreak of the Civil War. It was a delight to teach, in part because of its mix of nineteenth-century case law, literature, and American political history. It traced the constitutional crises around slavery that occurred with each westward act of American conquest. What were some of the core principles of the original constitutional text? How did its formation relate to the tensions within the American economy at the time, in particular between slave and free labor? How did the evolving political context of westward expansion, from the original states to the shores of the Pacific, force continued reinterpretation of the constitutional text?

We were going to read James Madison's secret notebooks from the Constitutional Convention in Philadelphia, along with the classic, thousand-page chronicle of the political conflict around slavery, David Potter's *The Impending Crisis*. We were going to read antebellum case law and selections of contemporary literature from Herman Melville to Victor Hugo.

The most interesting student that semester was a short, thin, twenty-two-year-old African American named Lloyd Adams. For most of the other participants, who came from New York City and its metro area, coming to Greene was a double opportunity within the grim geography of punishment—access to the college program and a chance to move closer to home, with the result including a higher chance of visits from parents, wives, children. But for Lloyd it played out quite differently. Since he was from western New York state near Syracuse, his acceptance of the DOC's offer to move to Greene for the year meant relocating *farther* from home.

What else did I know about Mr Adams? Someone had diagnosed him as "learning disabled," which was recorded in the DOCCS files that we had been given on students at Greene. At Eastern, and at all other BPI campuses since, we have viewed state records on the academic backgrounds of our incoming students very cautiously. Students who wanted to share such concerns with us are free to do so, but we typically choose to leave that up to them and allow the college to encounter its new students with a clean academic slate. Lloyd then was diagnosed with something that was supposed to make him difficult to teach, or to disqualify him from the kind of college opportunity Bard offered. (We have since met any number of good and even outstanding students through BPI, who have volunteered information about the presence—and consequences—of past diagnoses of this kind.)

I had prepared the syllabus to introduce students to the constitutional framework in some of its fascinating complexity, but I found I needed some simple materials to provide a basic narrative introduction to the events. I wanted a "simple, clean" introduction to set the stage.

The college's classroom at Greene, as it turned out, was normally used for mandatory GED training. Sifting through the materials lying around, I came across a state-generated textbook covering the basic requirements issued by the New York Regents' requirements for the state high school exams.

I was shocked to find a narrative eerily similar to what I remembered from my own public school education on the topic in suburban Philadelphia twenty years earlier. Apparently, it was still being taught that the major controversy which divided the framers was the conflict between big states and small states—those with large populations, like Virginia and New York, and the smaller ones, like Rhode Island or South Carolina. Further, this was presented as a purely technical power-sharing "deal" that needed to be struck by influential big states and less populated small states. The tremendous impact this deal had on the character of American government, and the profound limitations it imposed on democracy, are ignored. And most notably for my class, the most controversial issues of the convention, as noted by James Madison himself, its leading figure, were excluded.

I distributed copies and we walked through the conventional narrative, as retold by the GED materials we had accidentally inherited in our classroom. If states had a voice proportional to their populations, big states would dominate and the small states would never agree. The solution, as we had been taught in public school, was the "Connecticut Compromise": a Senate with states represented equally, two senators each—regardless of their population—and a House of Representatives where population mattered, and something resembling one vote per (white, male, propertied) person. This was a regressive and antidemocratic structure by today's standards (and opposed by contemporary democrats like Ben Franklin), but a fairly moderate compromise for its time. The Senate, then, which empowered regions and locals, was profoundly antidemocratic, as was the linkage of House seats to a geographic district, as was the election of the president by an "electoral college"—all features designed to protect governing elites and part of the core political geography of the eighteenth century.

We spoke at length about how, at the heart of the Federalist vision, lay a desire to constrain the powers of the state, of government generally, by subdividing its institutions in a mode of thinking central to the eighteenth-century liberal tradition. The goal was to protect the liberties of citizens, for Madison and his colleagues feared majorities as much as they feared kings, and they had a powerful concern for minority rights. Partly this idea had much to do with their wish to create something that could survive, a form of republicanism that would overcome the fatal conflicts of factionalism by balancing them out and channeling them. This concern has evolved over time into one of the most compelling elements of the American political tradition, but we think of it in ways that strip its richer—and more problematic—meanings. In Madison and the other framers' eyes, the most vulnerable minority faction needing defense from an imagined tyranny of the majority was the wealthy—owners of any and all forms of property. Because those who owned more would always number among the few. Inequality of wealth was taken not just as a fact of life, but as a sign of justified political entitlement. The defense of the propertied elite thus lay close to the heart of Madison's and the other framers' concern for minority factions and fear for the powers of majoritarian democracy (which bands together those who own less). This concern led to the antidemocratic safeguards created in the Supreme Court, the U.S. Senate, and in the separation of powers.

The GED textbooks were still teaching the big-and-small-states story, but stripped of all that makes it interesting—and controversial—today, namely, the wish to structurally defend liberty and good government by structurally defending the minority of groups and persons that controlled the majority of property.

Lloyd spoke up. "Earlier you mentioned that we would use what you called 'primary' and. . . . was it 'secondary' sources. Is that right?"

"Yes," I answered.

"Well, this one you introduced as a secondary source."

I nodded.

He smiled slowly and continued, somewhat amused. "But now the way our conversation is going . . . it seems to be interesting because it's still the same way of talking about it today as it was back when you were in school. And if what we're saying is that it's important for what it *doesn't* tell us . . . what we don't even get taught today . . . well, doesn't that make it a primary source?"

I smiled in turn, and acknowledged that he was utterly correct. It was produced by its authors, and sought out by me, as a secondary text, intended to introduce a topic from the past and summarize its history. But, based on our interest in what it said about those who had written it into today's public school curriculum, it had become a primary source.

"About what we do and don't teach today," he concluded, reminding me of Friedrich Nietzsche's assertion that history is a record of what has so far been kept silent.

"Mr Adams, if you're writing that sequence of thoughts down in your notebook—would you mind preparing that for the next class? I mean summarizing what you're thinking right now, and presenting it back to us the next time we meet?"

He nodded, but didn't look up from his writing.

"Now, here would be a fun project. You could compare how this particular history is taught in public school systems across the country. Is it taught differently, say, in Massachusetts, or in different counties within New York, or in southern Virginia, or wherever? Or over time in the same place? You could look at that too, and try to think about why such things might change."

"Or not change," he said, still buried in his writing.

We finished up class with two different quotations. The first was from the founding father John Jay's eloquent summary of his Federalist vision: "The people who own this country ought to govern it." These words electrify students today. They were axiomatic for eighteenth-century political liberals, but are typically expunged from today's public textbook narratives, as if our social contract is today too fragile to sustain the most interesting controversies and questions that should be the lifeblood of a political education. In class, we contrasted this, for the time being, with the words of Abraham Lincoln, on the campaign trail for the U.S. Senate fifty years later. Summarizing in his deft frontiersman's retail way the updated ideology of the Republican party, Lincoln said: "We are for the man and the dollar. But if forced, we shall choose the man *before* the dollar."

It was a great class—we explored the text and some of the context of the Constitution, but also touched on the writing of history too—the way that subject was taught and retold, and what was included and what was kept out.

FOR THE NEXT class I asked students to read the Constitution closely and identify all the sections that referred to the institution of slavery.

Students came back with nothing—not a single word or phrase.

Lloyd was particularly frustrated with his failure to discover anything about slavery in the document. "Why did you ask us to do this assignment if there's nothing in there? Are you wasting our time?"

Another student added: "We already knew those men didn't think twice about slavery and were fine with it. So why ask us to look?"

"Fair enough," I answered. "It's true, the term 'slavery' appears nowhere in the final text of the Constitution."

"And nowhere—" Lloyd interrupted, "nowhere in the GED materials."

"Yes. So the silence of the framers on slavery in the constitutional text resonates today in the materials prepared for all of us when we go to school—or, at least, when we're stuck somewhere completing a GED. And remember—the Convention at Philadelphia was secret. The men who gathered at Independence Hall were sworn to secrecy—banned by mutual agreement from sharing a word of what was being discussed and debated behind closed doors."

"That's not in the school materials either," someone added. "Whoever knew it was secret?"

"No, it's not in the GED materials either," I said, "even though it immediately makes us all want to know more! It's a great inspiration, isn't it? It would make a lot of students really want to know more. But I was never taught that either. Isn't that a disappointment? It would have been troubling. It would have been really interesting. Tricky, controversial maybe, but interesting.

"So. Back to secrecy. Why might the framers have decided to impose upon themselves a vow of secrecy about the Constitutional Convention? And was that a good idea? Was it justified, do you think?"

"It's fucking antidemocratic," another argued.

"Yes, it's fair to say that it was fucking antidemocratic. Look, these men thought of themselves as statesmen. Let's consider it from that angle for a moment."

"Sure, it was a good idea," Lloyd interrupted. "I can see that. If they talked in secret, they could say what they really meant." Lloyd always spoke very, very slowly, but his ideas seemed always worth waiting for. "There's often times when you know you can get more done if you do it on your own—you know, without folks listening in."

"I can sympathize with that, too; perhaps many of us can. Now get a load of this. That vow of silence was broken. And it was broken by none other than James Madison himself. For Madison, it turns out, kept notes—close, detailed, verbatim notes—word for word, of the proceedings at Philadelphia. Worse than that, he didn't destroy this record when the Convention was over. He kept them his whole life, in secret, in his personal library. He never destroyed them."

And then I read them the following words from the private notes Madison took during the Convention at Philadelphia: "It seems now to be pretty well understood that the real difference of interests lies not between the large and small but between the northern and southern states. The institution of slavery and its consequences form the line of discrimination."

Another student broke the silence. "So where'd that come from, if you said Madison never let it out?"

"Great question. They were published by a young, iconoclastic Harvard law student and radical abolitionist named Wendell Phillips."

"When?" another asked.

"He published them in the 1840s—half a century later—when the country was in the midst of a great struggle over slavery. As we'll be studying this semester, they were debating whether or not slavery should be extended westward as the young, empire-building United States was taking over the continent and expanding toward the Pacific." I continued, "There were a number of antislavery voices, in the North and even in the South as well—people opposed to the spread of slavery as the country spread westward. But they were okay with its staying where it already was, and of having existing business continue as usual. But Phillips was a radical, a secessionist—although not the kind we normally study. Actual abolitionists were a tiny minority among white Euro-Americans, and they were radicals. They felt that the Constitution was irreparably flawed, and that the Union, founded on the alliance we're currently studying between slave-economy and relatively free labor economies, had to be dissolved. That it was so broken from the outset (morally, that is) that it couldn't be fixed. You can see that we're headed in this direction, by looking ahead into the copies of the syllabus."

We were out of time, and we turned to the assignment for the next class.

"So we haven't really gotten yet into the text of the Constitution, and why it appears silent on what Madison called it's most important issue—the issue over slavery. Let's try again. Review the quote from Madison's secret record from Philadelphia; look through the rest of the Constitution again. Then read the first chapter from Finkleman. Good work. See you Thursday."

THE NEXT CLASS began with a summary of what we'd covered. According to James Madison, the single biggest issue threatening to divide the Convention, frustrate the framers, and destroy the prospect of a national constitution was slavery: the clash of economic interests and moral vision that divided representatives from free labor states and slave labor states. The text of the Constitution as written in 1787 quite simply cannot be meaningfully read without a thorough exploration of this topic.

As we spoke, the door to the classroom opened unexpectedly. A uniformed officer stepped in, followed by a familiar official, nervously frowning at us in our semicircle. He in turn was followed by a slew of state officials, all male, all white, and all in suits.

Someone among them said, "We're just here visiting the pilot you all are up to. Carry on, and don't mind us." The dozen or so anonymous men from the state capital's Central Office stood along the sidewall and watched.

They had not arrived to hear our reading of the civics classics drawn from *The Federalist Papers* No. 10 or 51, or our review of the theories of the framers as sketched by Richard Hofstadter in *The American Political Tradition*, or our open-ended discussion of a selection from Alexis de Tocqueville's *Democracy in America*—above all, those beautiful passages where he writes of his sense that democracy and the progress of modern history shatter the great traditional chains of being, freeing men from their fixed place within an endless line of ancestors, but leaving them, as a result, alone and adrift to face their fate in solitude. No, they were walking into our discussion of the most the racially charged parts of the original U.S. Constitution.

The students seemed unfazed by the presence of our unannounced visitors. Perhaps they were so used to being observed and surveyed that nothing about this struck them as remotely unusual. That bothered me—for if our classroom was "different," then in part this meant that it was a space where they felt *less* surveyed. If they felt little difference in the classroom with the officials in it or not, then what did this say about how I considered, or romanticized, my college space?

"Okay," I went on, "so we're discussing another variation on the theme of how the historical record is made, how our primary texts and secondary narratives are always a function of what is included and excluded."

I paused, and the class waited.

"And we were talking about why we couldn't find the term 'slavery' in the Constitution, despite Madison's report that it was essential to the drafting. You've also seen that some of the most important figures there, including the southerner and slave-holder Washington, thought the institution of slavery would die away naturally, under the pressure of free trade and competition between inefficient forced labor and efficient free market labor."

"May I read this aloud?" Lloyd interrupted.

I nodded, and glanced over at our guests. "Yes, where is this from that you're reading?"

"Some of it's from that encyclopedia thing you gave us, and some of it's from Madison's notes."

"Ok, great."

Lloyd read aloud:

On Saturday, August 25, John Dickenson moved to make the slavery clauses more explicit by changing "persons" to "slaves." Several delegates objected to this. Madison records his own objection.

"Then next it's—they quote that other guy," he went on.

"One second, Mr Adams. Who is 'they' and who is that 'other guy'?"

"They—that's this encyclopedia thing. Then the other guy—that's Phillips. Or no, Madison. They quote Madison."

"Ok, thanks."

So Lloyd continued, and read this aloud:

Mr Madison thought it wrong to admit in the Constitution the idea that there could be property in men.

"I guess that's Madison in his notes referring to himself as Madison," Lloyd clarified.

"Exactly."

"And then it's they," Lloyd, who was really getting good at all of this, went on, "who wrote the encyclopedia—they write:

> A draft of notes that Dickinson made for a speech at the convention (but which he apparently never gave) arguing in favor of using the word "slave" included this statement: "The omitting the Word will be regarded as an Endeavor to conceal a principle of which we are ashamed."

Another student broke in loudly: "Leaving that out—that was pretty much the same as just a lie. This guy Dickenson was right on—they were ashamed—and they was also probably too deep in it themselves in the business to take that on. So they just left it in, and left the whole slavery thing just keep right on going."

"I agree, it was a kind of lie," Lloyd said. "But I think it was a good thing to do—to keep it out."

"If they'd put it in, they'd had to actually face up to it totally," the other student pressed.

"Yes, but then it'd have been in there forever—in the Constitution. And maybe some like that Morris wouldn't ever have signed it," Lloyd said. "And if folks like Washington thought slavery was on the way out, then they may have thought the Constitution was the best way to limit it, and drive it out faster. I can see that."

I let that exchange sit for a moment, then Lloyd asked me, "Did the abolitionists, later, did they think it was right or wrong to have left the word out?"

"Great question, and I don't know the answer."

"Well, Phillips thought it was a bad idea," Lloyd added, answering in part his own question.

"Yes, that seems right. An expert historian of the period, perhaps someone else on Bard's faculty, could give you a better answer than I, but I think your reasoning there makes sense. But it's a great topic for further study. Let me just point out that among us here now, there are a number of different views about whether or not it was a good idea or not to consciously keep out a clear reference to such an absolutely crucial institution—slavery—from the final text of the Constitution itself." I said, "Just as there was, it seems, disagreement in the room in Philadelphia. I also want to acknowledge how the two of you are disagreeing. You're reading closely. And note how Mr Lloyd acknowledges right off, at the start, *where the two students agree*, before he goes on to add or clarify where he disagrees. That's superb. Thanks to you both for that—for all of that."

"Says here," Lloyd added, "Dickenson 'wrote' but 'apparently never gave' that speech."

"So the one guy who wrote a speech to *include* the word, never even gave it?" the other student asked.

"Yes," said Lloyd.

"And he was an antislavery guy. Wanting to shame them or something," the other student added. "Well, obviously, that room was very different than this one!" he said, laughing.

At that moment, our official guests began to leave, filing out through the door as quietly as they had entered.

◆

"Take possession of that which you have inherited."
—Goethe, *Truth and Poetry*

FROM HIS INTERVENTIONS in class, Lloyd impressed me and his classmates as a thoughtful and gifted student. His increasingly assertive dignity and insightfulness were unmistakable. Like the others, he had no formal education beyond what he'd received in a few years of public schooling. Labeled by experts as in need of special education, he'd since completed a GED, his credits cobbled together over periods of juvenile and young adult institutionalization.

Lloyd's life seemed woven in patterns of innocence and experience, and I read both worldliness and parochialism on his broad face, as he perhaps read them, likewise, on mine. A youthful vitality could be felt in the way he carried his large frame, along with a jaded, premature weariness. I imagined that he had a lot of experience, but was not in the habit of sharing and articulating for others its significance.

A few weeks into the semester I received word that Lloyd was requesting to leave the college program. He had requested DOCCS officials to withdraw him from the college pilot and move him to a prison closer to home for the duration of his sentence.

Having heard the news, I came to our scheduled meeting at office hours afraid that he was going to abandon what I thought was one of his lifelines to a better future.

Lloyd sat before me in the whitewashed room, below a bright, barred window. Beyond the window was a seemingly infinite series of other walls, fences, razor wires, and watchtowers. The student was not much younger than I, and the closeness in our age exaggerated the gaps between us riven by class, the experience of race, and so many other aspects of our lives. As we sat together, I realized that I should check my impulse to encourage him to stay in the college; I knew nothing of his motivations or of the pressures that might lead him to such a choice.

Sitting at a shared desk, he explained to me that the grandmother who had raised him had died suddenly several months ago. She had hidden from him the gravity of her condition, so it had been too late for him to apply for permission to attend her funeral, let alone to see her before she passed. With a certain odd consistency of vision, officials often permit inmates to attend the burials of the loved ones from whom their incarceration is designed to cut them off. Now word was brought that his father was dying. The college had been dear to him, he explained, an extraordinary opportunity. He made it clear, in his reticent eloquence, that he had tasted something that was somehow right for him. He also knew, he said, how many thousands of men in prison had been excluded from the seat in Bard's classroom that had somehow fallen to him when prison officials selected him to join. But he could not stay here, in the middle of nowhere, to wait while his father died back home.

I asked him if he had been close to his father. He said he had not, and that, to be honest, the man was dying of alcoholism and had been remote from him as far back as he could remember.

Would his father be well enough to visit him in a prison closer to home? No, Lloyd said, probably not. Had they corresponded much, since his incarceration? No, they hadn't (though prisons are places full of writing, as if the isolation and technological deprivation leads to all sorts of writing, journaling, and correspondence). Lloyd added that he used to write and send letters to both his father and his grandmother, but the older man was not one for writing. He had never expected written replies from either of them. This father, he suggested, was all that remained to him of his immediate family.

Lloyd and I sat perched atop the small, plastic school seats that DOCCS provides in all its classrooms. He held himself with dignified resignation and fixed my gaze as we spoke. Here was a man whose circumstances were so remote from my own, but whose steady engagement and keen intelligence in the classroom we shared made me feel a professional allegiance with him as a teacher.

Sensing or imagining what was at stake, I took the liberty of directly addressing my concerns. I said it was terrible that his grandmother had died while he was so far from her, that he had been moved around from prison to prison as punishment for something he'd done, and that this loss, and this particular way of separating from a woman who had meant so much to him, was something he would have to contend with for a long time to come. I told him, also, I could understand that, despite his father's long absence from his life, it was all the more difficult to bear. But, I said, going to a prison closer to the dying man's hospital seemed to accomplish nothing. He was right to say that the college opportunity, seen abstractly through the numbers of men eligible and tiny handful "permitted in," was a precious thing to sacrifice. But it was far more than that, in regard to his own position, and who he was. I told him that he was obviously very bright, and that I was certain he recognized this himself—when he heard the sound of his own voice in the classroom, when he sensed what stirred inside of him as he was doing the readings, alone, holding the book in his hands.

"Where does this talent, this potential that you have, come from?" I asked. "In part, surely, it comes from your family, from all the people who came before you and who have contributed something to who you are, and who you might be."

I was shocked to hear myself say these things, and I watched him watching me. I rarely stepped across into such a direct personal appeal with a student. I wanted to respect their privacy and the college space where they themselves should be able to control how and when that space was "personally" significant to them. A professor or administrator should not foist that onto the meaning of their education. I felt I should teach what I knew, and what I was trained to teach, and to defer as much as possible beyond that to the students themselves.

"This talent of yours," I went on, "it comes from your father, it comes from your grandmother—and as remote as they are from you now, as cut off from them as you are, this is with you, is part of you, and is inside of you now. It's your inheritance, you could say, and the sort that nobody can take away. Pursuing college, finishing these few last weeks here, getting through and completing this is the greatest tribute you can give to them. Doing this for yourself, for that part of yourself that comes to you from them, is the best thing you can do for them, and the only way, really, that you can give them something back."

Lloyd listened but spoke little. This may have been due to the limitations in my own approach and abilities as a teacher or advisor; perhaps I had misunderstood what he needed or wanted. Or he may simply have preferred to keep his thoughts to himself, since the topics were too personal and lay well beyond the topics we had come to work on together in class.

All I know is that he thanked me and shook my hand warmly before we parted. Several days later when I returned to Greene for class, Lloyd was there, and stated matter-of-factly that he had decided to stay.

He continued to flourish as a student, studying assiduously and continuing to read and speak with insight. As an increasingly engaged member of the class, he nevertheless facilitated the speech and participation of others in the group with whom he had found himself, at random, in that flawed and fleeting year of study.

Lloyd wrote increasingly well and at times brilliantly. As the class progressed he became less interested in the legal and constitutional texts, and more engaged with Frederick Douglass's *Narrative*. Ironically, his final piece of writing for the course was a remarkable essay about what we might call the political geography of Douglass's life story.

Douglass's *Narrative* is a brilliant example of the nineteenth-century *bildungs* tradition—stories of self-development that link the hero's struggle for purpose and self-realization to a larger engagement with social change or political emancipation. In class we had touched on this theme, by way of the nineteenth-century progressive theory that societies evolve in history away from relations of "status" (like caste or slavery) and toward relations of "contract"—based on individual agency and mutual agreement, an idea made famous by the English jurist (and colonial administrator) Henry Maine.

In his final paper, Lloyd traced how Douglass's physical journey, as recounted in the autobiography, seemed to mirror not only his own personal development, but also the progress from slave labor to contract in a free market. Indeed, in his own telling, Douglass began life in the lower South and moved successively north, to the upper South and then North. Along this physical journey, he gained the opportunity in the border country between North and South to work as a hired servant, entitled to the surplus of his earnings after the share expropriated by a master. He thus entered a quasi-free paid labor under conditions resembling the economic and political ideal of contractual freedom envisioned by the nascent Republican Party. According to Lloyd, this northward progress was further woven into Douglass's representation of his literary life—first, learning to read and write from materials outlawed under slavery, and culminating in his successful career as autobiographer, in London, and later, back in the United States, as an editor, speaker, political figure, and diplomat.

◆

"*Contraband*: anything put to use for something other than its originally intended purpose."

—common prison usage

At the end of the year the students picked Lloyd to speak on their behalf.

We were to hold a modest ceremony at which participants were to receive their certificate—a faint echo of the "last graduation" that I had somewhat controversially discussed at orientation ten months before. This small ceremony at Greene was shielded from the outside—there were no family members and no press. Its small audience consisted of those who lived or worked behind the walls. It culminated with the presentation of a certificate of the sort that is printed in florid typeface on mock parchment, they simulated a level of social distinction or prestige and in doing so typically indicated the opposite.

The ceremony, however, was taken as seriously by the graduates as any of the similar events that I have come to participate in since, on conventional campuses or inside prisons around the country. Perhaps it was the moment of dignity associated with the cultural capital of higher education; perhaps it provided a fleeting opportunity for someone like this young man to speak formally in front of those who operated the establishment charged with his confinement. The ceremony might even have stood as a testament to a brief, fraught period of promise that had somehow taken place in the midst of his incarceration.

That morning, Lloyd stepped up to a small podium, to tell the story of the first college course that he or anyone else in his family had ever taken.

He began with the standard niceties: "I would like to thank everyone from the college who made this happen, and all of my teachers who came inside here to teach when they didn't have to."

Anxiously, my eyes moved over to some of the prison officials sitting with me in the front row, as we heard Lloyd continue: "Each of these classes has been important to me—Professor Rosenberg's literature class, Professor Demian's anthropology class, the writing course. I would in particular like to thank Professor Daniel, who taught a class called The Constitution and Slavery."

These words gave me an anxious surprise, but also flattered my teacher's vanity.

Lloyd continued at the podium.

One of the readings in that class was Frederick Douglass's *Narrative of the Life of a Slave*. In it, by the way, one of Douglass's masters is a man with the family name of Lloyd. That's my name, my father's name—Lloyd.

In the *Narrative*, Douglass tells the story of how he learned to read and write, which at the time, under slavery, was a crime. It was a capital crime, punishable with death. But Frederick Douglass, as a child, had a teacher—the wife of one of his masters, who began to teach him how to read and write. One day the master discovered his wife teaching the slave-child the alphabet. Very angry, he calmed down enough to explain to her that these lessons had to stop. *"Give a nigger an inch,"* the man said, *"and he'll take an ell."*

Ell. That was the white farmer's way of pronouncing elbow, an old way of measuring the length from a man's hand to his elbow. Douglass, I thought when I was reading his *Narrative*, was looking down on the man who had once called himself his master. The lessons ended—the master shut them down. But in his book Douglass goes on to tell all about how he took what he had learned and went on with his own education, and how, among other things, he would trick other neighborhood boys, white boys he played with the streets of Baltimore, to correct his spelling and, by "proving him wrong," were tricked into helping him further along in his own education.

Well, I wanted to say here this morning, that with this year of college here at Greene, I've been given an inch—and I intend to take an ell.

Lloyd was asserting himself into a series of speakers whom he could now trace back to a Maryland farmhouse in the early 1830s thirty miles outside of Baltimore. On the page, an utterance of this sort might be italicized or placed inside quotation marks; but to capture the full resonance of its spoken lineage, the currency with which it has moved from one speaker to the next.

The result is sometimes a tribute, sometimes an attack, and it is always charged with irony. In his autobiography, Frederick Douglass had taken the words of a former master and made them his own, tracing their violent genealogy and radically transforming it. Lloyd in turn was appropriating and transforming the words of Douglass, an author he had come to know as an adult, on intimate terms and under extraordinary circumstances. Out of the circulation of such utterances the world is made, undone, and remade; and it is really only out of appropriation that a person enters into a voice of their own.

Lloyd drew from a close reading of the literature, and situated himself in a process in which he, perhaps for the first time so self-consciously, believed himself to be playing an active part. It also seemed to enact what Peter Bay's interview would later suggest to me was why many men pursue the college inside the prison: to participate without giving in; to accept, and incorporate, without submission; to refuse to run away; and to take on the risk of applying oneself and risking both success and failure.

His use of our most charged and contested terms to identify himself with Douglass was risky, I thought, playing on the loaded subtexts that filled the room that afternoon. It may have been intended to stir up solidarity among his fellow students and also, perhaps, to provoke the rest of us, an audience overwhelmingly white, including prison officials, the Bard faculty, the guards, and myself. At the time, his inflammatory words felt inappropriate. And, sensing I was an intermediary between the students, the college, and the prison system, I felt that some would find the parallels he drew between the world he had been born into, the place he was currently incarcerated, and the institutions of slavery excessive, even outlandish.

Watching Lloyd standing at the podium at Greene, surrounded by official representatives and fellow faculty, I felt that by invoking slavery he was implicitly covering up or minimizing his own personal responsibility, or, perhaps, that others in the room would hear it this way. Lloyd's performance, then, enacted the tension at the heart of much of the most critical thinking on criminal law and punishment—what William Connolly has described as the right's "insistent model of individual agency" conflicting endlessly with the left's "insistent model of social causality." In drawing our attention to the structural injustices of our systems of criminal justice, an utterly essential critique, was Lloyd not also shifting attention away from personal responsibility for his own actions? This, at least, was how part of me felt, and—just as importantly— was how I imagined that officials in the room heard it.

In my complicated position as an administrator, within but not of the prison, beholden to it, in partnership with it, but also duty-bound to our students and the independent liberal arts vision of the college, the audience that day loomed large in my imagination. My own ambitions for the college depended on their good will and the ability to bring together teachers and students like Lloyd himself on terms the prison system could find not only tolerable, but also worthwhile. I had institutional investments, alliances, and ambitions from which it was impossible to disentangle my own readings of Lloyd's words.

But it was also surely his place to assert what he wanted to say on this remarkable occasion, and, having been called on to speak, he was free to negotiate the circumstances as he saw fit. And surely Douglass's narrative was a superb text for such a production, as one of the most remarkable American invocations of the power of intensive reflection, reading and writing to refashion an individual identity and transform a republic. For that charged moment, Lloyd had been called upon to literally perform his education in prison, and he had done so by treating with skill and care the very texts and tools that had been at the heart of his year of study.

As we had discovered in the conventional curriculum that year, it is a common travesty to teach the origins and significance of the U.S. Constitution without engaging deeply with the place of slavery in the founding of the country, its central place in both its economy, its fundamental law, and its contemporary ramifications. In a similar way, I have long noted how our familiar but quite important moral imperatives for individual responsibility and culpability all too often serve to conceal and displace the political imperative, equally important, to take shared responsibility for the foundational and deeply flawed institutions that constitute so much in our selves.

The somewhat bumpy experiment at Greene was coming to an end ten months after it had begun, and that day's ceremony was its fitting culmination.

CODA

About twelve months after that certificate ceremony we received a note indicating that Lloyd had called while we were out of the office. It was the first time in the brief institutional life of the Prison Initiative that a prisoner—a student, now released, now at home—had called us.

He left a phone number but no message. A quick check of public records confirmed that he had been released from prison. I kept calling the number back, which was for a listing in Syracuse. On two occasions it was answered by a woman of indeterminate age who listened in silence as I introduced myself and explained that I was from Bard College. Each time she uttered a word or two about taking a message, and then hung up on me.

Lloyd had made his one call to campus three months after his release. We never heard from him again.

CHAPTER 3

Going to Class

READING *CRIME AND PUNISHMENT*

LLOYD'S EXPERIENCES ARE a reminder of some of the ways that the work of BPI and its students is strongly informed by racial inequality. But race does not define or limit that work. Liberal education allows each student to analyze race and other pressures of structural inequality in the learning that unfolds. This is by no means a question of being free from or transcending race. Education cannot be "free" from the problem of race, quite simply because it takes place in America, and in prison, and because the purposes of a liberal education lead us to seek out and confront precisely such features of experience.

The same is true for the relationship between BPI and the punitive function of the prison. BPI is shaped by the prison's machinery of punishment, but the relationship is ambiguous. The college does not take clear sides on the tension between a moral commitment to individual culpability on the one hand, and a broader structural critique of punishment and criminal justice on the other. Both are woven into the fabric of the college as an institution and a way of life. Its role, partly, is to serve as a catalyst as students take personal charge of framing and answering such questions for themselves.

The ethos of the college as a public space enacts a rich politics of interpersonal respect and care that resonate with fairly conventional norms of civility, restraint, and personal responsibility. At the same time, the college's critical practice encourages serious inquiry into the foundations of existing moral conventions and the structural injustice of the existing criminal justice system—and many other key concepts and institutions that make up the world we live in. As a result, the college stands between the state's apparatus of judgment and the individual's subjectivity, reenacting certain norms and challenging others. The college's place "in between" is what Peter Bay began to describe at his interview, from his perspective as a thoughtful applicant confined within the prison but still on the margins of the college. What the college meant to him was directly related to the sort of introspection that accountability should spur; but he also thought that liberal learning offered him a markedly different approach to both personal introspection and outward confrontation than the prison did.

BPI typically engages students convicted of serious and often violent crimes. In this sense, as noted earlier, the student body is indicative of most of the people in New York prisons. And in some important ways, an education based on principles of dignity and respect, which addresses incarcerated students as students exclusively, amounts to an intervention in the moral economy of punishment. For some, this intervention serves as a reaction to one of the more cynical voices paraphrased at the opening of the book: yes, people do change, and yes, a proper response to crime in a democracy must include the maximization of future-oriented opportunities for change; and yes, liberal education's commitment to change is an essential part of the optimism that defines democracy. For others, the implicit meaning of the college in prison goes further, suggesting a critique of the moral foundations of punishment itself, of how individual culpability is understood and acted upon by the punitive state, especially under existing social conditions that include, among other features, the racialized nature of mass incarceration.

A college like BPI can never transcend the coercive power that defines the prison within which it works. As a result, it cannot avoid the distortions that this power asymmetry imposes on the ideals of a liberal education. Yet as students confront, analyze, and navigate these features of the college-in-prison landscape, they make the mode of liberal learning deeper, and maybe more impactful, than it is in more conventional, or less challenging, situations. Managing BPI involves not only commitment to the dignity of each student, but the frank recognition of, and respect for, the inequalities that mar every encounter between students and the faculty and others who represent the college. Together they and the college must cultivate their differing but shared identities as scholars; but this entails also a nuanced if mostly tacit recognition of the fundamental facts of incarceration. In practice, this often means that faculty and advisors resist students' desires to draw the college into the prison's workings, by often refusing to play the role of social worker or advocate—choosing the moments at which to do so with great caution. The temptation to be drawn into the details of the carceral experience are legion; the rewards for resisting it are often vast, above all for the students themselves. The result is a space that opens up between the prison and the individual subject of criminal justice, in which the students pursue their education on a middle ground that offers expanded opportunities for independent free-thinking, self-invention, and collective enterprise, as well as confrontation and dissent.

BPI is misunderstood if it is placed within paradigms drawn from criminal justice or religious transformation. This point only became more explicit as BPI helped to launch other programs around the country. More broadly still, what BPI suggests, most interestingly, may have little or nothing to do with prisons: it suggests we can and should rethink the opportunities for serious study for a wide range for people chronically cut off from the best of American higher education. BPI works by giving people a place to be and become serious students, and all that implies. It is at once within and removed from their immediate environment, keeping much of the "prison" at bay, on the shores of an island of liberal arts college established within, allowing the prison and its contexts back into the flow of learning by way of the students' changing, self-defining interests and the demands of the various academic disciplines. BPI is not primarily "about changing people in prison." It suggests, rather, how we might change the landscape within prisons themselves. As one of my colleagues who is helping to build a sister program in the Midwest has noted (he is a first-generation American, a Catholic monk, and a virologist), the college in the prison is stable and successful precisely because its relationship to students is narrow but deep. It offers neither to "change" bad people, nor to dismantle mass incarceration. BPI is powerful, transformative, and at times controversial—but also and precisely *because* it is limited, modest, and even, in a sense, conservative.

The previous chapter explored the necessity—and limits—of a racial analysis of BPI, by tracing the vicissitudes of students, teacher, and administration in the midst of a class on the Constitution and slavery. Here I explore the importance and limits of a criminal justice analysis of BPI by tracing a class on the law and humanities devoted largely to a reading of Feodor Dostoevsky's *Crime and Punishment.*

By the end of 2004 BPI had grown significantly. We had ended the partnership at Greene but partnered with other officials to open projects on the Eastern model, first at a medium-security prison for men called Woodbourne, and we were preparing to begin classes at a women's prison called Bayview in Manhattan. Eastern became Bard's thriving central campus, where we offered the AA and were well on the way to offering the BA. Students would eventually begin their college careers at Eastern, and would then transfer to Woodbourne as their security level "dropped." This meant they could move within the system toward release while remaining continuously enrolled with their college until they went home.

Several of us were increasingly preoccupied outside of the classroom with administration and policy, and Max and others we had brought on board as colleagues were managing the ever-more-complex relationships with state government and private philanthropy. As the college program grew, it remained among our highest priorities to maintain our stubborn attachment to individual students, supporting them through academic struggles up through graduation. Over time this would mean negotiating with the Department of Corrections to hold students in place or to return those temporarily lost due to "movement," or to disciplinary problems that had nothing to do with college.

Bard's courses in prison increasingly reflected the full breadth of what was offered on the main campus, embracing mathematics, computer science, genetics, European history, South American literature, foreign languages, and we were growing to meet the needs of students as they advanced from the AA to the BA.

As BPI grew, my courses in law and the humanities played an ever-diminishing role in defining the character of the program. From the beginning, though, my courses had been outliers in that they seemed at first glance to "fit" in prison: Justus's course at Greene on global literary genres or others on Nietzsche across the disciplines, or Charles Darwin, or cultural anthropology had been far more typical than my course on the Constitution and slavery. (Another of my staple offerings was a class on civics that was, in part, about the place of classical liberal thought in the American political tradition.) I had developed all of my classes long before I had any involvement in prisons, creating them for either the Rhetoric Department at Berkeley or the Political Studies Program at Bard. But the topics and texts they engaged did at times resonate directly with the prison as a site of study, or, by extension, with the situation of people studying inside, and this is precisely what made them rather unusual, to some degree both at Bard and within BPI.

"Law and Literature" was to be one of the last classes I taught for BPI before I was more deeply drawn into other aspects of the work, such as building a network of similar programs around the country. The bulk of the course involved a close reading of Dostoevsky's *Crime and Punishment*, focused on the book's nineteenth-century context, its symbolic structure, and the intricate devices Dostoevsky used to show the interplay between consciousness and conscience—which he imagined as an unending series of internal and external dialogues.

Published in twelve monthly installments in 1866, *Crime and Punishment* was a best-selling page-turner. It portrays the aftermath of a murder committed by an indebted law student named Raskolnikov, who kills his pawnbroker and her sister. The novel turned the conventional murder mystery on its head by showing the murderer and his method right up front in the novel's early scenes—dispelling at once the matter-of-fact mysteries of "what," "who" and "how." In their place, Dostoevsky created a spiritual mystery about motive and guilt. The drama is driven by what goes on in the heart and mind of the killer—and his conflict with an innovative police detective, trained in the nascent field of psychology or the "science of soul," who eventually secures the young man's confession. Dramatic scenes of cruelty and compassion are set in the impoverished urban world of nineteenth-century St Petersburg and its tenements, back alleys, taverns, and sordid police stations. Its cast includes prostitutes, pawnbrokers, and informers. A novel of action and character, of suspense and intellect, its characters debate everything from Christ to revolution.

At the heart of the novel is a conflict that wracked pre-revolutionary Russia: modernity's challenge to traditional religious views about sin, freedom, and crime. To echo the words of the contemporary American philosopher William Connolly, Dostoevsky set out to attack the "left-wing . . . model of social causation" that was as popular among Russian nineteenth-century socialists as it is among today's progressive reformers. Although he held onto some of the Christian socialist passion of his youth, the mature Dostoevsky had become increasingly devout and czarist, defending a conservative model of individual action grounded in a transcendent relationship between God and conscience. Dostoevsky set out to write a popular crime thriller that would also defend the Christian foundations of conventional approaches to crime and punishment from radical secular and socialist criticism.

One Thursday afternoon that winter I was scheduled to teach "Law and Literature," but once I had made my way through security and the long walk to the prison interior where the school lay, the clerk, Dezi, who was also in the class, met me with a bright, nervous smile. He wanted me to know that most students had been prevented from coming up to the school. He was generally anxious, dedicated, and cheerful. Behind his bright and even ebullient demeanor he always seemed beset by troubles he kept to himself. Dezi was one of the most dedicated students, and his warmth felt genuine; but so too did the weight he silently carried. Students in prison must be listed on official rosters or "call-outs" in order to be summoned to move from the cell blocks or the yards up to the college area within the school. That afternoon, the call-out lists were lost and most students were unable to attend. A handful of students with flexible job assignments or other privileges had made their way up to the school without the formal call-out, and none of us wanted to waste the opportunity of being together.

Five or six of us—including Joseph, Daryl, John, and Dezi—improvised a conversation in the library. We sat around rectangular desks made at a prison factory farther upstate. The desks were heavier than they looked, on folding tubular metal legs, their wooden veneer trimmed with a brown vinyl band. The students had pushed a group of these desks together to form a large, common, seminar table, where students outside of class gathered to study, tutor each other, and hang out. It was the central gathering spot for the college inside.

Dezi, sporting a closely shaved head, was one of the most enthusiastic and gifted of the AA students at Eastern. When he had first applied to the college, his application essay had been a mess: it ignored the text given as a prompt, and it showed little patience or sense of the expectations associated with close reading of an academic text. Beyond this, it read like the work of a person still mastering English as a second language. Although he wasn't accepted to the college, Dezi took a spot in our informal "college prep" course. A year later he reapplied. In the interim, he had clearly worked very hard. The second time around, he had more or less won a place in the incoming class on the strength of his essay alone. At the interview, he described the great effort he had put into mastering English and practicing his skills as a writer over the year following his initial denial. He spoke of how much that rejection had meant to him, of how seriously he had taken it to heart, and how he himself had known that he wasn't ready. In the year that followed, he devoted himself entirely to preparing. Dezi glowed with pride at his achievement and excitement at the hard work that lay ahead of him in the college.

That winter at Eastern, Dezi was working on a paper comparing two of the most entertaining and problematic characters in *Crime and Punishment*—the law-student-turned-killer, Raskolnikov, and his mysterious double, Svidrigailov. Dezi was particularly interested in the suggestion, made at several points within the novel, that Raskolnikov had somehow killed himself, or come close to killing himself, in killing his victim, the pawnbroker Alyona.

In sharing with us a detailed portrait of these parallel characters, Ricardo referred to Svidrigailov's "natural depravity."

"Is that phrase from the novel, or are these your own words?" I asked.

"No, I don't think it's a quote. Those are my own words."

"So what does it mean, Dezi, to say that something—say, a trait that someone has—is 'natural'?"

"It suggests to me," he said, "that it doesn't come from anywhere—that is, that it's from inside."

"All right. Now in class we discussed the distinction between a 'strong' and a 'weak' claim. Would you call that claim—that someone's depravity is natural—a 'strong' or a 'weak' claim?"

Nobody answered, until Hisham, an upper-level student who was listening in, spoke up from across the library and declared, with his characteristic certainty: "It's an incredibly strong claim, obviously. What could be stronger?"

"I'd tend to agree, Hisham," I said. "But Dezi? What do you think?"

Before we could continue, Daryl jumped in and added more slowly: "And it's a strong claim in part because it suggests that it's impossible to change it."

"Excellent. Let's hold that subject of 'change' very much in our minds. It lies at the heart of Dostoevsky's interest in confession, in struggle, in suffering. Recall the secondary readings on redemptive suffering in the Christian education Dostoevsky received so intensely as a child?"

I continued, "This idea of change is relevant to thinking about conversion or redemption, which are big themes as we near the end of the novel; but there are, of course, secular versions of this idea. The president of the college, back on campus, likes to say that a belief that change is both possible and good explains why education is so important in democracies."

"People say 'natural' when they also sort of mean God," Joe added from the other side of the table. "Could you speak more to that? It's not entirely clear."

I paused to think of how to draw out Joe's thinking on this, when Daryl replied.

"People when they say 'it's natural,' they often mean, well, just that it's *good*, like, 'don't criticize this, because it's *natural* to do this or that.'"

"That's *very* true," John nodded.

"But other times," Daryl went on, "sometimes people use the word 'natural' when they're feeling something like 'God made it this way.'"

"Yes," added John, "that second—or third—meaning, that's what I was thinking of. And they're kinda fused, like, the logic is: 'It's good—it's natural—God made it that way.' Though with Svidrigailov—that would be different. It's like it's bad—it's natural—it cannot be changed.'"

"I love it," I added. "This term—'natural'—is *loaded*. Let's pause to back up. We can arrange claims that we make—empirical claims that aim, or claim, to simply describe how the world is, as well as moral claims that judge the world, indicated a judgment about what is good or bad—we can arrange both sorts of claims along a spectrum from strong to weak," I said. "By that we mean the strong claims are very sweeping, or ambitious; while weaker claims are more modest—attempt to say a little bit less, about fewer things. So it seems from our discussion that this term 'natural'—on both the empirical and moral aspects—is quite a *strong* claim: whether we use it to describe something or to judge it as good or bad. Indeed, to claim that any phenomenon is 'natural' can often be one of the strongest kind of claims that people make."

Dezi, after a long silence, spoke again: "This is about the relationship between who he is and what he does."

We all let that sit for a moment. Hisham had put down whatever he'd been reading and stood watching from across the room. When nobody else spoke, I continued.

"Let's draw out on a piece of paper a range of alternatives to the term 'natural' as a description of Svidrigailov's depravity."

One student said "spontaneous," another "accidental," another "social," and another "habitual." More terms were added, and the students played with shifting them around along a spectrum of strong to weak claims to describe an action.

In the midst of many comments lost in the swirl of conversation, Hisham and Dezi, after a back and forth on the matter between themselves, pointed out to the group that habits are both *social* and *acquired*.

We turned to the phrase "Svidrigailov is depraved." Joseph put that on the spectrum very close to "natural" and later brought up the religious saying he was raised with that distinguished "the sin from the sinner."

"Now regardless," I replied, "of each of our own personal opinions of that idea, of that profound commitment to the distinction between the act and the agent, what's important for the time being is to note where it sits along a spectrum of description and judgment."

John nodded, adding, "This is especially important for us."

"That may be," I replied. "You'll find variations on these ideas across theologies and the social sciences as well—wherever there is a description, analysis, and judgment of human action."

WE SPENT TWELVE weeks intensively discussing the novel. Never in those twelve weeks did I ask the students about either crime or punishment. Nor were they asked to draw on their own status or experience to engage the novel, or to speak as a particular subset of students about their experiences of crime, its social contexts, or their punishment. Despite the book's title and subject, their own personal relationship to these issues was never solicited. Nor were they ever asked to remain silent on such matters, or to refrain from drawing such connections as they chose; they were simply never invited to do so, implicitly or explicitly. I have, before and since, taught the course both inside prison and on conventional campuses like Bard or Berkeley. With one or two exceptions, students in prison, just like other students in conventional settings, have chosen *not* to steer either class discussion or their own essays in such a direction, and they have preferred not to relate its central issues to themselves or their predicament in an immediately personal way.

During one of these class sessions I hosted a visit from the founder and director of "Network," one of the oldest rehabilitative programs of New York, based in the social service wing of one of the major Protestant denominations. He also became one of Max's earliest supporters just as Max was graduating from Bard College.

But his approach to the field of work was quite different from the direction taken by the college program he encouraged in its earliest days. His own program has been described as follows:

> [This program] rests on the therapeutic community model of behavior modification, a group-method approach that is recognized for its effectiveness in reducing drug abuse behavior. Therapeutic communities seek to build individual self-esteem and a sense of community among participants by focusing on personal responsibility for behavior and individual attempts to learn from and change that behavior. By confronting and examining its members' behavior, the group reinforces positive ways of thinking and acting consistent with those of the wider society (e.g., hard work or personal responsibility). The ultimate goals of treatment or recovery are changes in individual participants' lifestyle and identity. (Don Stemen, http://www.vera.org/pubs/network-program -episcopal-social-services-process-evaluation)

An ordained minister and an advocate on behalf of the incarcerated, this man, then in his late sixties, had been helpful in broadening the access that Max and the college had already gained inside the prison system. In his long career in corrections he has worked as a chair of the state commission on corrections (in the tumultuous era immediately after Attica). He had developed the Network Program based on the concept of voluntary "therapeutic" communities on inmates and the formerly incarcerated.

This minister sat in on a two-hour class during which we discussed the symbols, characters, scenes, and key ideas of *Crime and Punishment*. Several students were asked to give detailed summaries of the plot covered in the day's reading. Discussion focused first on the author's themes and techniques—the imagery of feeding and sharing food as a symbol of solidarity and alienation; the use of conversational ellipses and fainting to indicate the guilty man's moral and social condition; the wordplay associated with the pawnbroker's "pledge." Secondly, students spoke to the different and competing interpretive perspectives on physical illness and crime that each of Dostoevsky's characters gave: the medical student's interest in a moralistic neuropsychology; the radical's emphasis on material conditions and a rigid model of social causation; the young girl's emphasis on popular and deeply felt beliefs nurtured under peasant Russian Orthodoxy.

After class, the visitor commented on the tremendous opportunity that such a course presented. The inmates could reflect on and share their experiences as former violaters who were now part of a therapeutic community, transforming themselves into morally reflective individuals. Together, they could comfortably confess their wrongs and share their hopes among each other. This attitude was typical of "corrections" and other rehabilitative practices, with its heavy emphasis on the discourse of self and "changing the self."

It had never occurred to me, with my background in conventional university settings, to elicit such a response from my students, or to structure the purposes of the education in such a way. At the time, I found his question shocking, for it seemed to diverge so fundamentally from how the college approached its work, its various disciplines, and its students. I explained that I had never once brought up the subject and, in the open space this left in the classroom, not a single student had chosen to fill it with either a confession or even a direct grounding of their readings in a specifically "relevant" personal experience. Nor, of course, had I. More broadly, I said we felt that the inmates might seek out other, non-academic opportunities for such interactions outside of the classroom, and that the college provided something quite different—an opportunity to inhabit and excel in the role of student. From the earliest days, this had been second nature to me, to Max, and fit well with the ethos of Bard College. The longer I would be involved in BPI, the more I realized just how central this approach was to our work.

COLLEGE IN PRISON is divisive in part because we are still struggling with questions that preoccupied Dostoevsky. Conservatives among us tend to insist that individuals, imagined as atoms afloat in the world, must answer for their actions. Yet they perform this caricature of the human condition with a fervor that not only reflects the increasing harshness of our economic life, but that also recalls the satire of Nietzsche, who suggested that the individual was invented precisely because we needed someone to punish. Social-minded progressives among us tend to insist that individuals remain a continuously emerging product of structural forces, inequality, and our neglected collective history. For such critics, the turn toward the individual and punishment has less to do with justice and more to do with obscuring the very social facts that should otherwise drive political responses to crime. Liberals, all too often in my experience, do not have a clear or strong position between these two poles of thinking, although in criminal justice their interventions tend to focus overwhelmingly on a gentler, if not more effective, preoccupation with the single personal subject and the rehabilitation or alteration of his or her behavior.

In keeping with our legal and social culture as a whole, criminal justice embodies a worldview that is radically individualistic. It focuses on the individual crime, the individual victim, the individual perpetrator—and his or her culpability, containment, and punishment. This individualistic view marks not only the harsh, strong "right hand" of the state, but also the gentler, welfarist "left hand"—preoccupied with the transformation of the individual subject through any number of individualized and individuating exercises of institutional power: behavior modification, positive and negative incentives to reward "good choices," anger-management therapies, drug-addiction therapies, job-training programs—the list is endless.

The college has a unique role within this landscape. It engages the full range of our divided ideological loyalties without making peace among them. These loyalties—that can and should remain divided—lead the college, on the one hand, to emphasize individual choice, freedom, and responsibility. Yet they also demand of us a full recognition of the power of habitus and history, and the structural powers that forge the private lives within which our decisions, preferences, and desires are formed. Ethical relations between people demand a robust sense of individual responsibility. Political relations of power and citizenship require the assumption of social, collective, and historical responsibility. For all of their differences, both modes of thought and feeling are central to the complex ethos of a liberal arts college.

THE BARD STUDENTS who launched BPI flourished in a prison system from which liberal arts education had been largely effaced. But significant state money was still spent on "programs" in prison. Liberal arts largely disappeared, but correctional nonpunitive programming actually expanded. Money was not "saved," in the sense, but shifted. Vocational training and therapeutic cures replaced higher education. More recently, this space has also been occupied by evangelical projects that often merge, as the scholar Tanya Erzen has explored in depth, correctional and missionary objectives. Religious interventions in prison may be increasingly embraced by the political establishment that oversees state prison systems, by officials who see them as the most appropriate form of public-private partnership.

BPI's goal is not to provide a therapeutic space for prisoners to reflect on their transgressions. Nor is its aim to cultivate within them a belief that society has wronged them. This is what makes our mission, and our partnership with the state, so tricky. We want those in prison to find their own way through their education that will, however, if at all effective, lead them to a cascade of encounters with just such questions. This is what creates the greatest difficulties in protecting the integrity of the college, and education, while justifying its presence within the prisons. But working with partners in state government, this very worldview can often form the basis of the partnership between the college and the officials who support it, some of whom see the college as reflecting some of the best of the work they do.

How one conceives of this relationship between the college and the prison informs every aspect of the work. In the eyes of many, the college and the prison fit well together and make an appropriate institutional partnership: both seek to form character, alter subjectivity, and direct and control behavior. From such a perspective, the phrase "correctional education" makes perfect sense. And indeed, this is how the field is typically referred to. From state legislatures to the United States Department of Education and the major foundations, college inside prisons remains too often a creature of correctional, rather than educational, policy. It is envisioned and measured by criminal justice metrics, not those drawn from higher education broadly, let alone the liberal arts.

Too often, college faculty enter from outside and fit comfortably within the daily operating incentives and long-term correctional goals of the facility. Both can take the reduction of recidivism as their common measure. This lack of distinction between education and the prison becomes a greater problem the more structural or official the program is. Where public funding—and the correctional approach to policy—shapes the vision of college inside prisons, the opportunity for the college to stand between the state and the subject of incarceration is often compromised, or lost. Often the lines between correctional staff and college faculty are blurred or merged. Working together, they can jointly execute an inmate's long-term "reentry plan," tailor the content of courses, and efficiently control the "dosage" of postsecondary correctional education.

This blurring of progressive education with state correctional policy is perhaps what the increasingly conservative Saul Bellow referred to in his novel *Humboldt's Gift* when he mocked the liberal establishment's embrace of college in prison in the 1960s and 1970s: "Education has become the great and universal American recompense. It has even replaced punishment in the federal penitentiaries. . . . The tigers of wrath are crossed with the horses of instruction, making a hybrid undreamed of in the Apocalypse." I share Bellow's dismay at the specter of such an alliance.

Like everything else, the college that enters the prison is transformed. The prison exercises a powerful force over every individual, group, and institution that passes through it. Do conditions of confinement—and coercion—distort and pervert the relationships between the liberal arts college and its students? Do they alter, or clarify, the meaning of the liberal arts? There is no easy answer to these questions, and they should continuously plague the educator who works with incarcerated students.

It must be recognized that the prison and the college have very different objectives and cannot, in fact, be reconciled. Practically speaking, if the college is to set foot, as it were, in the prison, it must also remain at arm's length from the prison, and the relationship must inevitably be awkward and inefficient—so that tension can and does remain. At the same time, the college must maintain conditions of mutual respect and trust between itself and the public officials with whom it partners on a daily basis, and upon whom its continued existence remains dependent. In the space opened up within this difficult and potentially conflicted institutional landscape, a person in prison may live, with great power and purpose, a life approximating that of a student.

SAMENESS AND DIFFERENCE

How much should such a college alter its structures and standards when reaching out to incarcerated students who appear so different—in age, current circumstances, social history, and academic preparedness—from its conventional students back on the main campus? Should courses be altered in pursuit of greater relevance to people in prison, and should the college, as an institution defined by avowedly ethical norms, explicitly address students as guilt-bearing persons, as convicted criminals marked with a special relationship to the liberal arts? Should the college redesign its basic requirements to respond or resist the carceral institution, viewing the college-in-prison space as a unique political opportunity?

Speaking about the sameness and differences between the Bard students enrolled through BPI and those on the main campus, the chair of anthropology at Bard shared an interesting anecdote. "My students on campus—what you all call my 'conventional' students," she said, "It's common for them to say in class, 'Well, excuse me, but I'm getting quite uncomfortable here.' For them," my colleague explained, "getting uncomfortable in class is a real problem. But at BPI, I've had several students explain that they found themselves getting comfortable in prison—and that they applied to Bard precisely in order, as they put it, 'to get uncomfortable again.'"

This is the merest allusion to the differences between BPI and conventional students that are real, important, and extensive. But BPI has declined to take the distinctiveness of the prison, and incarcerated students, as a guide when designing and implementing academic policy. It has sought to replicate the main college inside, with all of its faults.

This approach requires BPI to resist two temptations. The first, of course, is the temptation to adopt a criminal justice or correctional framework for how students and their educations are imagined. The second temptation is the desire to design an academic program out of the fact that the students are "subalterns"—actively pushed outside of the social, political, or geographical centers of power: the temptation is to approach the design of a college program in prison as an opportunity to make a distinctive political intervention, by way of the curriculum or pedagogy rather than through the distinctiveness, within the prison, of the liberal modes of education found on a conventional campus outside.

Many college faculty who are most drawn to work in prison are likewise most drawn to the idea of politicizing and transforming the college, tailoring it not only to the perceived needs and interests of adult, incarcerated students, but also to transform it as a self-consciously modeled act of resistance against mass incarceration, or the "carceral state." At times, this kind of intentional transformation of teaching from the conventions of the main campus reflect an idea that the prison—and students in prison—represent an opportunity: a chance to pursue and establish modes of education, ostensibly better or more democratic or more politically engaged than those they find available, or desired, or permissible on their conventional campuses. One professor I was working with, who sought to launch a college-in-prison program at his own university, complained at length about the oppressively "conservative" approach to teaching on the main campus, and the unimaginative and reactionary teaching styles and methods tolerated by the undergraduate dean of the university. The prison was sought out by this and other like-minded faculty because it represented to them a particular kind of opportunity, a site where alternative and more progressive or social radical pedagogies could be employed that were otherwise thwarted on the main campus.

This approach is distorted because it would seem to add to the peculiar isolation of incarcerated students, to increase rather than mitigate the degree to which they were cut off from the opportunities afforded on a typical campus. It would also seem to radically change the tenor and temper within which they were addressed by their college as students. As administrators and advocates, we at BPI emphasize the similarities among the students and the two branches of the college. Not because this is the whole truth, or the only truth, but because it is the institutional and rhetorical path of greatest resistance and therefore the one that must be given the greatest care when designing curricula or training faculty. The dangers of overstating the differences are greater than the dangers of overstating the similarities, and students in the "conventional" college that puts itself in this unconventional space will encounter and create for themselves myriad opportunities to pursue their interests as they seem them, and as they develop over time.

BPI's MODE OF education defines the character of its intervention inside the prison. It emphasizes objectivity over subjectivity, the concept of "structure" over the concept of "the autonomous individual," and the critique of concepts over the process of identifying and assimilating norms. This is a matter of emphasis and overt structure rather than a matter of purity, for this sort of college education is always also subjective, individualistic, and normalizing.

By an "objective" educational emphasis I mean a tendency to call on students to focus their attention on the objects of study—the texts, controversies, concepts, and narratives put forward—prior to reflexivity, to a reflection on their own individual subject position and its particular relationship to the material at hand. This approach to texts and their contexts defers overt reflections on the prison setting, or the life experiences, ethnicity, class, moral, and juridical status of the incarcerated students. They are not entirely excluded—certainly not from the writing process—but they are not given a heightened relevance due to the facts or condition of incarceration.

By an emphasis on the "structural" over the "individual" as categories of analysis, I mean that structures and systems are usually given analytic primacy across the range of the liberal arts curriculum. This distinction within the curriculum and teaching methods contrasts it with the dominant modes in which people who are incarcerated are addressed by the surrounding authorities. Such dominant modes tend to emphasize individual choices, individually oriented systems of rewards and punishments, incentives and disincentives, and the logic of personal transformation.

Finally, by "concept-critique" I refer to all aspects of the curriculum and practice that identify, analyze, and historicize concepts as part of an ongoing ethical and political critique. The social space of the classroom, and of the college itself, is largely dedicated to this process. The critique of concepts is paramount across the liberal arts curriculum, most notably in the disciplines of history, philosophy, and anthropology, but also in those traditionally humanistic fields that have been so strongly shaped by anthropology and the philosophy of history.

Prison education schemes obviously offer a way to engage the morally autonomous subject, the theoretically culpable subject, in ways that support the moral justifications for punishment. This may be part of why a significant number of prison officials embrace it in the abstract as a potentially valuable program to bring inside.

In my function as an academic advisor, a second-year student approached me for advice about choosing courses. Something his professors said about his work from the previous semester was bothering him. Various faculty members had told him that his work needed "to go further," or be "more in-depth." While his arguments were well constructed, they suggested, his arguments remained superficial.

I began by offering him a hypothetical example of a student paper that we would critique together in order to think more about the difference between "deep" and "shallow." I began by asking him to imagine the opening paragraph of a hypothetical student essay.

College is an interesting place. Many people find college interesting because of the diversity of the people they encounter there—no two students, and no two professors, are alike. I, however, am most interested in college because of the courses I find there. Indeed, each course, to me, is something like a person—unique in and of itself—and rather than being engaged by the diversity of faculty and students in the college—the people I meet there—I am struck by the diversity of courses that I meet there, each class as unique and fascinating as a person.

This, I suggested, was a perfectly good way to begin an essay. Then I went on with the hypothetical essay.

For example, consider height. Just as no two people are the same height, so no two courses are the same length. Some are short—lasting only fifty minutes—while others are long, and can go on for as long as an three hours.

The student began to laugh.

"Why are you laughing?" I asked.

"Because that's not what makes classes different from each other," he said.

"But it is a difference, surely?"

"Sure. I see what you're saying—it's a difference, but it's not 'deep.'"

"So what is a 'deeper' trait that might distinguish one class from another?"

"What goes on *inside* of the class—the subjects, the points of view, stuff like that," he answered.

"OK, so let's go inside that class. Our imaginary student continues her paper as follows. . . ."

For example, then, consider the arrangement of seats in the classroom. Classes differ in how the seats and desks are arranged.

The student smiled again and protested. "That's not what I meant by what goes on inside. I meant the actual contents—of the class—of what the teacher says, of what you read," he said.

"Yes," I answered, "but even mundane facts can come alive if you let yourself go there. Let's consider for a moment the possibility that this fact—the arrangement of the seats—which looks superficial, like the sort of thing you're trying to avoid—is in fact interesting, that it has some 'depth.' What might you be able to learn, or understand, about a particular class, based on how the seats in it are arranged?"

"Well," he thought a minute. "You can tell a lot about how someone sits in class. If they're slouching, or hunched over, they're not going to be getting much, but if they're sitting up, you know, focused and all of that, if they're clean and whatnot, then they are going to be good students."

"You've changed the subject."

The student looked at me puzzled.

"Think over what we've just been talking about," I said, "and think about how you've just shifted the subject from one thing to another."

The student thought for a moment, and nodded. "All right, yes, I see that. You asked about the seats—where they were placed—the desks and the seats in the room, in this room right here, or in all the classrooms in the prison, and I switched the subject to how individual students were sitting in them."

"Now *that* is really interesting," I said. "People's way of carrying themselves could surely be another topic of interest—but let's stick with the seats alone—since that seems especially uninteresting. How does the actual arrangement of seats in a classroom change from class to class?"

He noted, "Sometimes they're in a row—like now—all lined up, one next to the other."

"And facing?"

"And facing the board. And the teacher."

"Yes, great. And other times?"

"Other times they're in a circle, or in a half-circle," the student said, now more rapidly. He went on. "That's when we—when students in the class can see each other, and in those classes, it's true, we tend to—the teacher also seems to try and get us to—talk more to each other. To have more conversation, more class discussion. And that's a big difference in terms of what can go on in one type of class or another—the way we, the students, you know, relate to each other—in class and also, outside, when we're studying, in the yard, or working, or in the cell-blocks."

"Who determines how the seats in a classroom—let's say this classroom—are arranged?" I asked.

"Well," he answered, "the correctional officers. Or the teachers—the prison teachers. The rules of the facility." He paused. "Also tradition."

"Great. Now you're talking about all of these different things which influence the arrangement of seating, and of people, and of talk, inside the classroom."

"Parts of the structure," the student clarified.

"That's right, that's a great word for it."

"'Structure'? We've used it in classes," he said.

"So we started with a detail, a fact—the arrangement of the seats and desks and teacher and students in the rooms—and now you're drawing connections that make this student's hypothetical paper deeper than it started out."

After a pause, I took a certain risk in the interest of pushing the conversation one step further, coming far closer than usual to an explicit analysis of the environment and regime of the prison itself.

"Now let me throw something out there," I said. "Consider for a moment that 'Corrections' tends to focus on individuals. Let's say, on things like how each student sits in their chair—on what we might call questions of individual comportment. Different types of student: the attentive, the industrious, the lazy. . . .

In contrast, 'the college'—teachers, the syllabi, the subjects of the courses—might focus on *structure*, on emphasizing the concept of structure."

We both fell silent, and the student stared at me gravely, stone-faced. He smiled after a long pause, and dropping the formal posture we'd both been maintaining, he stretched his arm out on the school desk and lay down, resting his chin on his forearm, as if daydreaming. Suddenly he sat up suddenly, and, nodding, said, with a smile of gravity and pleasure, "Yes, I can see that."

"Ok, so here's a suggestion. I've made an assertion about the college curriculum and the concept of 'structure' and the concept of 'individuals.' Take the list you've brought of course offerings and the descriptions from the college catalogue and look them over. Come back to office hours next week, just before registration, prepared to discuss whether or not the course descriptions support this assertion or contradict it."

INDOCTRINATION

Skeptical allies often ask how the general population thinks about the college in the prison. Are those people who are in the prison but not in the college, hostile? Do they resent the selectivity, the fact that so few in any given prison or prison system have a chance to participate? Are they deeply suspicious of an institution like Bard and the forms of education—and assimilation—it seems to offer?

The last question is most interesting. Some students have resisted the college because they consider it an alien and hostile institution that is inherently suspect. Some have told me that for a long time they turned their backs on the college opportunity because they felt the institution was "white"—or worse, that it was nothing but a form of brainwashing, which would undermine, through illicit and dishonest techniques, the ideas and ideologies that may have supported their life "on the streets."

This idea—that bright, capable people in prison turn their backs on college opportunity because they suspect it is a form of racial, class, or correctional brainwashing—interests me the most because it goes to the heart of the academic enterprise, and the worldview or ideology inherent in the college itself, especially in a liberal arts college.

Later that semester, I was again in the general library room, this time at scheduled meetings to discuss students' papers outside of class. Dezi and some of his classmates were with me there again, but the room was also full with other groups of students coming and going, some of them from a calculus study group and others practicing second-year Mandarin.

Voices rose—at once serious and jocular.

"Where'd you come up with *that* one?" I heard someone say, and the group broke into laughter.

Curious about all the fun, I turned to ask them what was up.

They resisted, hesitant to explain.

Then Marcus spoke up. He was an especially accomplished student who was thriving in both the higher mathematics and Mandarin classes. He was on a fast track to his bachelor's degree. He had moved from another remote satellite campus to Eastern, after his security status had fallen from "max-A," a higher and more constrained institutional regime. He had been a student of Bard's, but far from the main campus; and he had only recently joined what we call the "main campus" at Eastern.

With a full audience of the room now, and emboldened by my own good humor, Marcus explained. "I'd like to see the microscope that could tell the difference between education and indoctrination."

"Can you, Marcus?" I asked. "Tell the difference?"

"Some guys in the yard—they *hate* the idea that you tell black folks how to speak, that you're gonna teach *them* your white English, when they know just how—well—eloquent they are."

"They have a point," I said. "There are perhaps as many languages at play at any given time as there are people talking—and dialects, and regions, and families . . . and they in turn shape the mainstream. I think America has a mainstream, a 'standard' of language, that's especially fluid—responsive to the changes a diversity of people brings to it."

"Yeah, okay," Marcus said, "but when *we* hand in our papers, and we write in the language we were raised in, you all correct it and say it's wrong."

"Yes, that's definitely true," I said. "We teach in SAE [Standard American English] and that's our standard for style, grammar, and so on. That's the dialect of the academy. If you're going to compete, you've got to get a handle on it—ideally, to become a virtuoso in it. But you know better than I do that you're switching codes—you learn *this* code and it's just one more—well—skill. And maybe it offers you things that the other languages—or codes—you use, do not. You could consider it just a version of being multilingual."

He looked at me, thoughtful but still skeptical.

I tried again. "There was a linguist—his name was Weinrich, Max Weinrich actually, and he was from Europe but he was living in New York during World War II, during the Holocaust—and he was giving a lecture on Yiddish, the old Jewish dialect of German, at an institute on West 16th Street in Manhattan. There was a debate about the scientific difference between a dialect and a language. And, at one point, a high school teacher from the Bronx stood up in the audience and said, 'You wanna know the difference between a language and a dialect? A language is a dialect with an army and a navy.'"

"Ha," he chuckled. "I love that."

"I thought you might. Well, I do too. So too would nearly every one of your professors . . . certainly the ones, ironically, who are busy correcting your grammar! So that's what we do when we grade for grammar. You wanna be able to switch into the code of the dialect that has the army and the navy. You can try to change the dominant dialect from the outside, as it were, and you will.

It's always changing, really. But anyway—you might also want to change it from the inside and the outside. By all means, master the code, if only to change it."

He was smiling, and then paused and snapped back into what seemed like an ironic seriousness. "A friend of mine in the yard. He's a guy who's studied a lot. He could totally get in, but won't join the college. He thinks you guys are—well, I won't repeat it."

"Feel free. I've got a thick skin. Who knows? Maybe what he has to say is worth considering. Or maybe he just doesn't want to submit to anybody else's judgment—least of all 'mine'?"

"He said you work for the jails."

"Well, we're here at their discretion."

"Would you say you work for them then?"

"It's a messy question that deserves a messy answer," I said. "The college has no right to be here, and, for better or worse, no right for people in prison—or anywhere else, for that matter—to go to college. If others don't turn the key and open the gate, we're not getting in. God knows they don't pay us to be here— for better or worse."

"That's not an answer," he said, smiling but also quite serious.

"My answer is that of course we don't work for the jails, and in my view that's a very good thing. But maybe in some other sense we do work for the jails, in the sense that they think we're doing something for them? It's not an unreasonable supposition. Why the hell else would they let us in?"

"And do you think that?"

"I think I need to worry about that question—just like you do. We might all be involved in this in our different ways—for our different reasons."

"You're a smooth talker, Karpowitz."

"That's why you put up with all my bullshit."

He got serious again, and continued. "My friend, this man in the yard, he says that the word for 'teach' and the word for 'doctrine' are the same: 'docere.' From the Latin. And it's the word for *docile*. So it's the same thing. Already they're telling us 'Hey, your behavior better be perfect, or we'll pull out of the college program and ship you out of here.'"

"Hm. Well the etymology sounds about right to me, but I don't know Latin." I answered.

They looked at me.

Years of working together on the college in there and they still found such moments of frankness surprising. I didn't know Latin, and his friend in the yard might very well have a point.

"Look," I continued. "What your friend says is worth thinking about. I like to listen to the clues and winks our language gives us. There's a lot of wisdom buried in those old roots. I've come across the same etymology your friend has. I've heard this argument before, and it sent me looking into the back of the dictionary, where they keep the old roots: they're all related, supposedly— teaching, doctrine, docile. Does the connection make sense to you?"

"Is that what we're doing here, then?" he asked me.

"You're answering my question with a question. I love that. Well, if the words themselves somehow speak the truth, if etymologies *are* the truth, then there you have it. But maybe this nexus—to teach, to indoctrinate, to make docile—are *not* in fact all versions of the same thing, but are variations on the same theme. Of course you can take a thing, like a word, to be identical with its origins. You can do that."

I paused and waited, but a further silence allowed me to continue.

"You can do that. Not sure you'd want to equate a thing with its origins."

At this point, for the first time, Joseph, a lanky man with a ponytail, spoke up: "You could have the same theory for people, too."

"Meaning what?" the other student turned to Joseph.

"You could think the same of people. That if you knew their origins, where they came from, where they've been, who they've been—then you'd know who they are. You can take any word, any idea and say that its past *is* its present. That if you know where it comes from—if you know its origin or its roots—then you have a privileged access to understanding what it *is*; what its essence is. You've discovered its secret truth."

"And how would *you* take it?" the other student asked Joseph. "I mean, you've obviously drunk the Kool-Aid here. You buy into this college thing. How would you take the fact that the root of education is indoctrination?"

"I'd take it as a warning," Joseph answered smiling. "Not the truth."

CHAPTER 4

The First Graduation

FIGURES OF SPEECH

IN THE LATE FALL of 2004, the time had arrived for the first graduation of the Bard Prison Initiative. It was to be a moment of great celebration, in which years of work and risk-taking by students and the college leadership were to reach their first official culmination. Indeed, for six years since Max had first started building the college at Eastern, the students inside the prison as well as the president and faculty on campus had put an enormous amount of faith in the vision that this was feasible and was, year by year, getting done. The graduation was to be a moment of truth, in which the students were to encounter for the first time the college in all its breadth as a living, present reality; and the institution of the college, with its assembled faculty and trustees, was to encounter its students at Eastern for the first time, face to face, to hand them their diplomas on stage. As the day approached, the exaggerated fear that many of us felt was a symptom of the risks that had been taken and the aspirations that had been conjured, in the hopes that the reality would come to pass.

Yet our first graduation would also expose what I take to be tensions within this work that cannot be resolved. Students would be compelled to enact conflicting roles as they prepared and delivered their graduation speeches as both scholars and inmates. They would perform their graduation on stage as adults in the presence of those who had raised them, and as parents themselves, in front of children of their own. They were independent men celebrating a major milestone, and a collective of students who had carried on so much of the work of building a new, terribly complicated, and ambitious institution. They also had to perform as incarcerated subjects calibrating the risks and rewards of every decision they were to make about what to say, how to behave; negotiating and enacting, at multiple levels of often painful self-consciousness, the performance of both their incarceration and their academic achievement. In the end, I was to witness one of the finest triumphs I've seen a student achieve anywhere, as a graduate turned his speech into an opportunity to reveal what the ceremony, and perhaps the entire undertaking of college in prison, was all about.

A degree is both a practical credential and a powerful symbol, especially to students who are the first in their family to go to college. And because a graduation is very much about the ties that bind one generation to another, the commencement's symbolism is intensified in prison, where success and disappointment, accomplishment and loss, are so closely intertwined.

Pervading all of this was anxiety—a sense of disbelief as the graduation approached. In an era where such programs had become almost nonexistent, Bard's students in prison had taken a leap of faith to devote themselves to their studies while relying on the as yet unproven promise that the college would and could deliver a degree to students in prison. With the relatively recent and vitriolic revocation of Pell funding from people in prison and the swift destruction of such programs that had followed, they had good reason at the beginning to fear that the promise would not be fulfilled. Many of Bard's first students had begun college in prison years before, during the Pell era, and had lost everything when the programs were taken away. They knew this level of the history first-hand.

Finally, it seems the degree was the only lasting symbol the students would have of their success and identity within the college for the remainder of their incarcerations. Though there was a promise of ongoing enrollment, there was significant uncertainty about the future. Thus the formal separation that such a graduation implies was loaded as well with a fear of loss, as they faced the possible attenuation of their status with the college, a potentially ominous state of affairs if the time and space of the college are as vital and restorative as they appear to be.

I have often heard students share a quotidian saying from their pasts that appears, on even the briefest reflection, to be quite extraordinary. Sometimes in an admissions interview or casually in passing, outside of class, a student would say something like: "My mother told me when I was a boy, 'Pursue your education—because that it is one thing that nobody can ever take away from you.'" At some point, I realized that nobody in my family had ever said these words to me; it would never have occurred to them to do so. These words can thus be read as a chilling trace of the chronic, multigenerational experience of loss and even expropriation.

As the day approached, the college showed its full elegance, bringing in flowers and banners, traditional college regalia, and booking the brass quintet that plays at all Bard commencements. Diplomas were printed in Latin, the trustees were assembled, the president prepared his address. Matching our campus ceremony as closely as possible, we conducted dress rehearsals, the students practiced walking up to the podium to receive their diplomas. We revealed more and more of the formality, seriousness, and frank luxury with which we approached this and every Bard commencement. Replicating inside the prison walls the grandeur and pomp of its normal commencement ceremonies, and in orchestrating a ceremony loaded with cultural symbolism, the college might inspire the graduates and their families. But it might also inflame the distinctions that often separate the supporters of liberal arts education, and college in prison, from those who have reason to distrust or resent them. But it was the tension, or conflict, between the different roles of the graduates—as members of their families, and convicts within the prison system—would define the ceremony's significance.

The partnership between the private college and the department was a mutually beneficial collaboration. Yet the dance between the college and the prison system was always tricky, given that their institutional cultures and missions so markedly diverge, despite the common ground upon which the college-in-prison partnership is based. The style and publicity of the ceremony put everyone on edge. For the first four years, the program existed somewhat under the radar of a skeptical governor, enjoying at best the executive's benign neglect. As a result, BPI did its best to avoid press and any nonvital traffic in or out of the prison that hosted us. We did not know quite what to expect and, as the excitement grew over the coming event, we sometimes feared that this first graduation could also be our last.

A few weeks before the ceremony, officials in charge of managing the complexities of the ceremony and the hundreds of outside guests it entailed decided to increase the allotted tickets to the graduation ceremony that each prisoner could distribute to family. At the same time, they excluded nonfamily members, regardless of how close the relationship to the graduate might be. This decision was intended to be quite generous, as the numbers of family members who could visit at any given time was normally highly constrained. But it put some students in the awkward position of having to exclude people who were extremely close, even sort of fictive kin, if they lacked the standing of a parent, child, or spouse.

Provoked by this and other pressures, Malik, one of our best students, said he would boycott the ceremony. Tall and angular, Malik had a long-time female companion who had stood by him during his prison sojourn. If she were considered a member of his family, as in practice she was, and were treated like a common-law wife, there would be space for her under the new and liberalized rules. Malik did not, in fact, have enough family members to use up his portion of the newly expanded quota, and he proposed to simply use one of his family spots to include this crucial figure in his life. From the administration's perspective, however, this would open a floodgate of potential other requests, which may have felt unmanageable. In any case, his request was denied, and he was faced with including some who were legally family, while excluding what may have been the most important woman in his life. I thought this would likely put intense pressure on preexisting fault-lines within the extended family.

The unusual nature of the graduation was like a funhouse mirror, enlarging and distorting everything that passed before it. For the students and their families it heightened the visibility of both success and failure; for Max, I think, and certainly for me it exaggerated the sense of the risks to which BPI was being exposed. It would reveal the full extent of the private support needed to partner with the public sector as ambitiously as we had, discreetly, for years. As the day approached, I also sensed a growing feeling among the graduates that to participate in this ceremony, which belonged to them but also belonged to the college and to the institution, was to appear to accommodate and publicly authorize the prison itself, complicating their already tangled relationship to the day and all it signified.

Four years earlier I had watched these men enroll in college, I had admired them as they allowed themselves to long for something precious and to commit to something that made them vulnerable. Participating required them to join, help build, and care for something that could be so easily taken away, as it had been before when it was publicly funded. To truly desire the college might be to yield further to the vulnerabilities of being in prison. This was especially acute in the early years of BPI leading up to this first graduation, when the experiment seemed so fragile and the memory of how college in prison had been so abruptly and violently taken away in the mid 1990s loomed so large.

Graduating inmates were going to deliver a speech at the ceremony, and these speeches were going to be the heart of the event. Technically—and in the spontaneous moment on stage—they were free to say whatever they wanted. But they, like Lloyd, would say their piece under the judging eyes of public officials who governed nearly every aspect of their daily lives.

This was a complicated moment. For my part, as academic director of BPI, I was responsible not only for giving them feedback on their speeches, but also for making sure the speeches were appropriately "politic." I was charged with being a mentor for the graduates as they confronted this moment of self-representation, as well as the implicit representative of the college's interests. I was to read the graduates' drafts as someone who had been coaching them for years on how to analyze, care for, and respond to texts. And, with a heightened concern for the relationship between the college and the prison on this most public of days, and being keenly aware of and accountable to the broader political climate that BPI was exposing itself to for the first time, I might also be acting as their censor.

On the eve of my first trip out to hear the drafts of speeches, the new rules about invitations were announced and Malik took a stand. He would, quite simply, not attend his own graduation. Max was going to learn more about the rules and how our students might manage the situation, while I would try to get Malik to change his mind and make the best of the situation should the rules hold fast. We did not want to mar the ceremony with the absence of one of the handful of first graduates.

On the long drive out to the prison, I reflected on how best to convince him. I genuinely wanted him to share in the celebration. But I was not sure how frank to be about the college's own institutional interest, which I took to be keeping him as a visible participant, active on stage. Inside the school area, I sought out

Malik to try to strike a compromise, maybe counsel him through the crisis so that he would not, in my view, inflict this harm on himself. In any case, I wanted to nudge him toward participation.

Malik was very bright and often very charming. He had a round face, wide-open eyes, and a brilliant smile that came from deep within. While he was a bookish person, he hadn't taken easily to the breadth of the BPI curriculum. But he was a talented actor and an excellent writer of short fiction. Accomplished authors on the faculty thought he should soon be publishing his work. On a campus like Bard, where the arts occupied such a central and privileged place, he would have thrived.

Malik arrived late. He nodded at me in an air of confident resolve, beneath which I sensed more resignation than stubbornness. I sat, offering him a chair next to me at a corner of the makeshift conference table, but he, in turn, declined to sit. I joined him standing—and throughout the meeting he remained at the threshold of the door, never entering the college room.

"So, I hear you're thinking of not coming to graduation," I said.

"Yes, that's right."

"Can you tell me why?"

"That's what I've decided."

I laughed, trying to defuse the situation by appearing less concerned than I was. I had resolved to accept as final his refusal to attend, to express my disagreement but to appear calmly resigned to his decision. I wanted to appear more interested in persuasion than pressure.

"Do you want to tell me more about it?" I asked.

The smile came, Malik's characteristic charm, but it came broad and sad with eyes averted and then directed back at me. He remained silent and made a vague gesture with his head. I did not say, "Why are you doing this to yourself?" And I did not say, "We need you," and what I would never say, but found myself thinking, "You owe us better than this."

Malik said, "I'm not going to choose between my fiancée and my sister. Simply no way. I've been through too much of this. Everything's like this. Everything. And they want me to come and put on a happy face?"

Malik mimicked a kind of happy face, intentionally minstrel-like and twisted in sarcasm. It flashed for an instant and was gone. His look turned sad, glum, and withdrawn, although this too struck me as put on. His virtuosity was alienating—intentionally so. How little had I been able to read him in all our past exchanges, and how incapable was I of telling which expressions were coming from the heart and which were self-conscious performances? It seemed that all of his states—theatrical, angry, mocking, charming, resigned, or bitter—could be read as genuine reflections of his state of mind or artful affectations. To what degree was my inability to read him due to my own ignorance, a feature of his life before prison, or more narrowly a function of the besieged existence he led inside? And if he was always quite self-consciously performing in my company, was this largely a function of his disdain for me or the college or an entirely reasonable way for a person of his high self-regard and miserable circumstances to manage the gulfs between us, two bright young men of roughly the same age?

Mulling this over, I tried to convince him of the sincerity of what, ironically, I truly believed—for in the face of his remote and even haughty disregard, I found myself performing as well. There are moments when we stand, as it were, outside ourselves, watching ourselves affect words and gestures—even though we know at the same time these words and gestures reflect the very things we do indeed think and feel. It seemed there was no longer any common ground between us. Perhaps, I feared, there never had been.

I started again, saying that from one perspective the way the seating was being managed was not unreasonable, despite the way it imposed a particularly sensitive burden on him directly.

He shrugged. To consider this argument would be to join me, to acknowledge common sympathies, to sort out a way forward for both of us. But, standing at the threshold still, he refused to enter either the room or the conversation. I sensed nothing for a moment other than the image of him as a man with a long life behind and stretching out before him, much of it in a prison designed to inflict its punishment in part by cutting him off from the family ties that were now, symbolically, at stake.

What did I want from him? I wanted him to shield his college from the conflict he was undertaking. I wanted him to do this out of a sense of loyalty to Max, who had worked so hard with Malik and the college to create BPI. And I wanted him to do it out of a sense of gratitude to Bard—marginalizing my own recognition that this was precisely the sentiment that I had mocked when it had come from the warden.

Perhaps Malik was one of the men in prison who rejected the idea that the college could ever be something held in common by its leadership, faculty, and students in prison. Maybe, as an African American who had converted to Sunni Islam, he disliked and distrusted Bard as a machine dedicated to processing successive layers of assimilation, as an insidious "outpost of progress." These at least were some of the thoughts I had, as my mind escalated the search for strategies with how to connect. I had met activists in the field, among them prison abolitionists, who resented Bard for a host of reasons (it was frankly reformist, it was privately funded, it practiced selective admissions, it refused to re-politicize its curriculum inside). Among these might be added that it seemed to them a process of middle-class or elitist cultural missionizing.

After a long pause he said: "My mother always used to say to us, 'You get your education. Because that's something that they can never take away from you.'"

I waited.

"Now who would say something like that?" he added. "Who would *feel* that?"

"Hmm," I answered gravely. "Someone who has lost too much."

"Someone who has had too much taken away," he corrected. I faltered and returned to the ceremony.

"You know, if it were up to us," I said, "you'd invite all your people, regardless of their official status. You'd invite as many as we could jam into the room. On most campuses, tickets to these sorts of events are in short supply—but here, under the circumstances—one would go to great lengths to include everyone the graduates wanted. And I know that you guys have to put up with this sort of thing all the time. The college has to put up with it a little—indeed, it's part of our business to do that. . . . But the point is," I said, "this graduation belongs to you as much as it does to anybody, as much as it belongs to the other graduates and their families. More even than it belongs to the college, which also has a stake. . . ."

He stepped back for a moment to consider me, perhaps if only to defend against me better. Or perhaps he felt contempt for my acknowledging that, in my view, the college had a major role to play, along with its graduates and others, in fashioning the event.

He smiled and said nothing.

I thought: *He is sad. At moments he seems gleeful, enjoying the fight, proud to inflict some harm simply through this act of refusal. But he's also in dismay. Perhaps he knows this fight is small and hollow.*

"You've earned the right to celebrate this graduation," I said.

He was quiet.

"So has your family."

That provoked a response: "I'm not going to divide them like that."

"They might understand . . . she might."

His eyes narrowed. "No. That is *my* decision to make. I would never ask that."

He wasn't entirely wrong—I thought I could see what all of this might look like to him. I set aside my sympathies while continuing to try and persuade him to change his mind. Couldn't he handle this problem differently? He should join us in making the college his own, the college he had helped to build, investing himself in it as the other students had, rather than taking up this self-defeating battle with a rule I considered not all that unreasonable?

Perhaps if I had directly addressed the college's interests in the matter, he would have found me more convincing. My instinct told me otherwise; at any rate, I did not.

"You know, I would never say that you owe us anything," I said, "It's just such a waste."

He looked away. "A waste. Yes."

And in that moment, while he looked away and spoke beneath his breath, I think I came as close to him as I ever had, or ever would.

"There's the Devil for you," he added. And this word, I felt at once, not only shattered that instant of proximity, but was meant to do so.

"What's that?" I asked.

I was hoping I'd misheard him, or that he was speaking in some flippant, metaphorical way. The words seemed charged, and they upset me—an indication of so much in his mind and life of which I remained ignorant, and which seemed to escalate in my mind out of proportion as I sought, and failed, to find strategies for connecting with him.

"There's the Devil in it. This sort of thing happens."

"The devil? You mean, like a real, actual devil?"

"Yes, that's my belief. The Devil is a figure in my religion. And all this sort of thing is wrapped up with its work. Hubris. . . ." I waited for more. "Whispering."

Again I thought I saw that odd mixture on his face—sadness and irony, provocation and resignation.

The bells signaled the end of the module, and we parted. I had gotten close, and I had gotten nowhere. I knew that there was far more at stake here for him than I could fathom.

As I drove away from Eastern as I had so many times in the preceding years, the car seemed to drive me, hypnotically, along the familiar winding road. I gazed again at the glorious countryside of the Hudson Valley and recalled the brutal prisons that rose up occasionally amid its hills. The bucolic but depopulated countryside, its shuttered storefronts, the college's growing traffic of faculty and resources. The private, cosmopolitan college, building its bridges to the inmates of this remote, state-run prison, itself typically staffed by families who had moved up only a generation or two ago from the immigrant boroughs of the city.

BPI was tying together, in a small, busy, spider-like way, the fragmented parts of the city's complex social life—Italians from Long Island, Hasidim and African Americans from Crown Heights, borscht-belt vacationers—that had been scattered upstate over decades of economic ebb and flow. The commencement would reveal and intensify the unique social mixing, and the jarring juxtapositions, that BPI brought about. How would the graduates—migrants from downstate of a different sort—address the eclectic audience that their graduation was drawing into the prison? And what was at stake for us, in the answer to this question, that they and they alone could provide?

SPEECHES

Four graduate speeches would be the centerpiece of the ceremony. The graduates would articulate what their education had meant to them, and each, in his own way, would approach the question of how it related to his incarceration, just as Lloyd, during his certificate ceremony years before, had done at Greene. Thus, at the heart of the graduation was a series of performances that would cut through the veil of BPI's overall approach to college in prison, its practice of "normalizing" the college experience as much as possible. It was part of the graduation's power—and risk—that it would thrust into the foreground what BPI, inside its classrooms, left largely implicit.

On that stage the graduates would share in an unusual kind of freedom, standing at the microphone with the auditorium's sound system projecting their voice in real time, with a moment's unobstructed access to a large and important audience. This audience would also include the guards and officials who staff and ran not only the prison, but also the entire system. Some might resent the commencement and the honorific trappings of a higher ceremony commemorating higher education. Others, who lived more in a discourse of corrections and rehabilitation, would be moved, believing that they were partaking in the best of what the justice system had to offer, feeling a renewed dignity and hopefulness in their own public service.

It was less than two weeks to commencement, and the day after my failed intervention with Malik. I passed yet again through the Victorian facade of the prison and was escorted to the school in the back to meet with Noble, who was scheduled to appear as the first of the four graduate speakers.

In writing his speech at Greene Correctional Facility several years earlier, Lloyd Adams had drawn from the coursework in "The Constitution and Slavery," adopting as his touchstone one of that class's central texts, *The Narrative of the Life of Frederick Douglass*.

Unlike Lloyd, who had gained strength over the year at Greene and had ultimately been chosen to speak for his classmates, Noble was full of confidence before he ever joined the college. A bold reader and a loquacious, compelling speaker, he was at ease with his fellow students. Men in the college gathered around him as friends, comrades, and study partners. He was like a character from one of Herman Melville's ocean voyages—short and round but nonetheless a visible, charismatic lodestar whose presence seemed to orient the room around him. The fondness and respect he enjoyed among the student body led to his being among the four that the entire graduating cohort had chosen to speak at the commencement. He was also extremely bright and had earned a very high GPA.

Yet I had been disappointed with him as a student. In his work, and in my frequent conversations with him both in and out of classes, I found a seemingly impenetrable wall around his learning. Despite his great grades, he did not fully engage with the authors and ideas he encountered. He could describe thoroughly and with nuance and analyze with significant skill. But he remained unmoved by other students, faculty, or authors, and never quite offered up well-elaborated views or arguments of his own. These, if and when he had them, he kept to himself; who he was as a student, as an intellectual person, appeared unchanged throughout his career with the college.

Some time ago, Noble had told me that he'd been raised within traditions of a branch of African American religious life known as the Moorish Science Temple. He had suggested that before joining he'd been skeptical of the entire idea of the college inside. I wondered if his religious and social allegiances had kept him aloof from a deeper engagement with the college long after he'd decided to join. Some of the ideas associated with the Temple movement—racial pride, strong talk of "uplift" and self-reliance, alternative origin narratives and forms of self-representation—may well have given Noble his stunning resilience and unflappable air of good humor. But perhaps it was these same sources of resilience that made him unreceptive to a college like ours. Although he was an exceptionally talented student, Noble never seemed to take to heart any idea he encountered with us, or to expose his own deeply held intellectual pantheon to the living process of his studies with the college. He never opened up this inner life as a tradition to be shared, critiqued, or juxtaposed with any other. (Had he stayed with us long enough, he might have chosen to do his senior thesis on the history of the Temple, as a way to engage it with the deeper life of the college.) Intellectual challenge seemed more a trial of wills than an intimate discovery; a test of just how much could be mastered on the outside and how much left protected and preserved within. Other faculty across the disciplines, despite his excellent grades at the AA level, had a similar impression.

Just as I was about to step into the study hall to meet with Noble, Joseph stopped me discreetly in the hallway. He eyed me with a peculiar air of sympathy, touched with a quiet, omnipresent irony.

"What is it?" I asked, with a sense of foreboding.

"Two more," he said under his breath, leaning his slightly toward me conspiratorially. His gentle smile seemed sympathetic but a touch condescending.

"Two more what?" I repeated.

"Calvin and Salvio. They're not coming either."

I gazed at this old acquaintance, who had been among our first students in prison and one of the most talented and intellectually appealing students I'd met anywhere. That was two more of our graduates down.

"Any connection?" I asked.

He gave a slight shrug and frowned theatrically. "Noble is waiting for you in there," he motioned to the general college room. Before I could press him further, he opened the door and showed me in.

Noble handed me the first draft of his speech and we sat down. We met as usual amid the clattering din of linoleum floor tiles, cinderblock walls, and steel furniture beneath a caustic fluorescent brilliance. The intensity of our exchanges, which sometimes devolved into a kind of matching of wits, could always generate an air of privacy between us in the midst of the steady bustle all around.

As I began reading he said that he had built his speech around the figure of Bigger Thomas, the main character in Richard Wright's *Native Son*. Bigger Thomas? My concerns about our vulnerability at the graduation came welling up again.

I read the draft through, then asked him to read it aloud. We timed it and considered different approaches to rhythm and cadence. He had a fine, resonant voice, his accents inflected with a mixture of Brooklyn and the South, and he spoke with elegant force.

"We are all Bigger Thomases," he read aloud, practicing with me as his audience. "Each of us here has taken a stand as to how we would define ourselves. Each of us has rebelled against constraints that threaten to snuff out the meaningfulness of our lives. We are rebels making a radical statement, in all our vulnerabilities, in all our ugliness, that we believe in and are willing to invest in the higher potentialities of ourselves and the human beings around us. We are not the beasts of yesterday. We are not a collection of mistakes, failures, and disappointments. We are resilience. We are what remain after the storm has cleared. We will not accept labels that rob us of our meaningfulness. So to the fearful, I say: 'Our voices will not die or be killed, but will be written again and again and again and again. Thank you!'"

The speech was eloquent, rousing, and provocative. I liked everything about it—except the invocation of Bigger.

Noble was making explicit one of the most important features of the upcoming commencement—the contest over representation that had led up to it and would culminate, for a moment at least, on stage. He spoke to how identity emerges passively, as if out of the formative images we receive of ourselves through others' eyes; but he celebrated also how conscious self-fashioning and self-representation are possible, and that the graduation was an act of self-possession and re-formation. In the charged and often paranoid environment of the prison, these were courageous and important subjects. There is something uniquely forceful when a man held in the grip of such a powerful institution raises fundamental questions about it in public, offering up full-throated answers.

Yet I was also nervous. How would this speech be perceived— not by me, or the other graduates and their families—but by the rest of the audience, like the college's guests and influential state officials, whom it was also my job to imagine? The more I thought about it, the more my concern settled not on the content of his talk, but the symbolic standard bearer he had chosen, Bigger Thomas. Here was one of the most controversial and racially inflammatory figures in the cultural canon: the iconic "Negro" from American Communist protest literature, our literary tradition's most notorious fictional black killer. In a spasm of fear and repressed resentment, Bigger had suffocated the white daughter of his middle-class employer in her bedroom, and then dismembered her body to conceal his deed. On the run, and in a kind of compulsive haze, he rapes and murders his own girlfriend. Exposed through actions that in part betray his own guilty ambivalence, he is sentenced to death.

Was this really the image to use on this most sensitive occasion? For Noble, perhaps yes; for myself and the college (and hence the students as a group as well as all those who would follow in their footsteps), I had my doubts.

Wright had presented his Bigger as demonic and guilty of terrible crimes; but also as one driven by cultural compulsion (the novel's ultimate section is called "Fate"). Wright used Bigger as a symbol of the "natural" outcome of the American inner city, a creature of the spiritual distortions imposed by the country's long racist history and its ongoing economic and racial humiliations. At once grotesque and sentimental, his crime and his punishment make him a martyr to the corrupted society that had produced him. Perhaps this was an important variation on the "natural depravity" we had discussed around the conference table during our law and humanities seminar, for in the traditions of literary naturalism, society itself is the most important force shaping the human world, the effects of which could be studied, measured, and, potentially engineered. But at the commencement, I feared, the figure of Bigger would incite more than it would illuminate.

There was indeed nuance to Noble's use of the symbolic Bigger, and to his choice to identify himself—and his fellow graduates—with him. For he was offering up the graduation as a counter-symbol, indicating that the graduates had overcome, through their studies, the "fate" to which Bigger had succumbed. But I felt anxious that all the nuance would be lost, leaving only the shock of this dramatic invocation of the terrifying Bigger. Only the most confrontational subtext would remain: the outraged symbolism of Bigger Thomas, a wasted youth whose tragic death sentence, like the murders and rape he committed, served above all to condemn America for its institutions of racial servitude and criminal punishment.

I felt that the speech would do better without Bigger as its leading symbol, but when I began to suggest this to Noble, and to explore his thinking on the matter, I found that Bigger was little more than a symbol for him as well.

"How did you first encounter *Native Son?*" I asked him.

He smiled. "Daniel, I know that you all read it in your Civics class."

"Well, actually we didn't read *Native Son* in Civics. We read James Baldwin's critique of it. Baldwin felt that that kind of protest novel had become part of the problem."

Noble said nothing.

"So I'm just asking you to think about that—both as you so rightly draw attention to what your being up there on the commencement stage really *means* to you, and also as you make use of the famous 'Bigger.'"

Nothing. So I went on.

"Baldwin greatly admired what Wright had accomplished in that novel. You know he named his whole collection of essays after Wright's novel. *Notes of a Native Son.* In particular the essay about his own father, a very religious and very violent man. . . . But even in that gesture, one senses Baldwin's criticisms of Wright and the icon he had brought into the literary canon—even in that title, one hears Baldwin's irony, his critique."

But Noble hadn't taken that class. Perhaps his skepticism had kept him aloof from a class named "Civics," with traditional overtones of assimilation and haughty, "Anglo-Saxon" American exceptionalism. Of course, my class had been something quite different: an in-depth critique of the American liberal tradition, as well as an exploration of what one author on the syllabus called the symbiotic history of inclusion and exclusion that makes up our always-contested, ever-changing citizenship. But I at least wanted Noble to reflect on how "Bigger" existed for Baldwin, whom I felt was the greatest writer on America in the twentieth century, before Noble threw Bigger out into the crowd on commencement day.

"I didn't take that class, Dan," Noble reminded me. "But I talked about it with my man Joseph."

He smiled, and his words flowed with ease and confidence, tumbling casually. "They all talked a lot about that class of yours. And he and I talk through all sorts of ideas, books and all, everything, and that piece, that whole, you know, set of ideas really struck me kinda strong, and Bigger relates a lot to us, and I thought I'd elaborate my own perspective from there and that set of ideas."

"This is a courageous piece of writing. It's really good and I'm impressed. Perhaps it'll be fruitful to talk it through further a bit."

I was getting the disturbing feeling that he hadn't read either Wright or Baldwin.

"If you recall reading Baldwin, Noble, you'll see that he was deeply critical of Wright's novel, even angry. Baldwin is *angry* at America, for, among other things, its ongoing stupidity about the subject you write about so well—the power of figures, of representation, and the past. But while Baldwin was of course primarily angry with America, he was also disappointed by, angry with Richard Wright, the leading African American novelist who came before him. Baldwin is angry about Bigger Thomas as a literary creation and as a . . . as a political device. In part, it's the very power of Bigger as a symbol that enraged Baldwin. He thought Bigger was a caricature—"

I stood up from our table and pulled a college copy of Baldwin's *Notes of a Native Son* from the library shelves. I thought of asking Noble to read aloud, but then thought better of that and read it aloud myself. I tried the following passage:

> Recording his days of anger [Wright] has also nevertheless recorded, as no Negro before him had ever done, that fantasy Americans hold in their minds when they speak of the Negro: that fantastic and fearful image which we have lived with since the first slave fell beneath the lash. This is the significance of *Native Son* and also, unhappily, its overwhelming limitation.

Noble listened but said nothing.

"So this passage indicates Baldwin's great praise for Wright's accomplishment, but also his concerns. What are these concerns?"

"I don't know," Noble said. "But what I'm saying is different—I'm not sure those details matter. I know pretty clearly what I'm trying to say. Don't you think it comes across?"

"Yes, I do. But in your speech you only make one connection to the college—to the actual, interior processes of the college. And it's by way of reference to Bigger—the contested symbol of Wright's novel. So yes, I think we ought to get a handle on it. Here, let me read another passage, one of the hardest ones. It's difficult, but worthwhile. I think you'll like it, and you might find it could make your speech stronger."

I continued to read Baldwin aloud.

> . . . it was precisely Wright's intention to create in Bigger a social symbol, revelatory of social disease and prophetic of disaster. I think, however, that it is this assumption which we ought to examine more carefully. Bigger has no discernible relationship to himself, to his own life, to his own people, nor to any other people . . . and his force comes not from his significance as a social unit, but from his significance as the incarnation of a myth.

Reading these lines aloud, I admired again what Baldwin had achieved. I have never encountered a modern writer who, at his best, is more brilliant.

"What do you think?" I asked.

"Deep man. Good stuff. He's great. That's what I'm getting at too. You know, the myths people have about us—which I say even as I know very well the things that many of us have done."

Noble turned his eyes toward the draft he had presented to me and began reading his own speech. "We are not the beasts of yesterday. We are not a collection of mistakes, failures, and disappointments. . . . We will not accept labels that rob us of our meaningfulness."

"Yes, I see that. It's precisely this 'incarnation of a myth' that you're resisting—or replacing with another, more appealing one," I said.

It was clear that Noble had not read *Native Son* the novel, or Baldwin's essay about it, or Frantz Fanon's, which would have appealed to him perhaps more than either of the others. It was also clear that he had no interest in doing so.

Noble's speech gave all the attention to the performance of defiance—occupying the stage, donning the robes, raising the diploma in the air. He said nothing about the hours and years of substantive hard work in which these acts and performances were grounded, the interactions between students and texts that was the lifeblood of the "college." Without this substance, were the defiance, the self-assertion, not *mere* performance? Mere myth?

I was not bothered that Noble, like Lloyd, did not want to engage directly at commencement with his own role in the events that had led to his incarceration. This was not the place for confession, or declarations of remorse and promise elicited before a parole board. Such exchanges struck me as largely worthless, capable of producing a travesty of speech under conditions of coercion and extreme inequality. But I did want Noble to take seriously his deployment of "Bigger," and the meaningful work of the students upon which their graduation was based. I not only feared—perhaps irrationally or unjustly—the provocation; I resented what seemed like near total disregard for the processes of reading and thinking through texts that seemed to go along with it. This feeling was intensified, because such speech-writing is a very important process, as they articulate what the college has been about, often by way of an engagement with a text from class.

"Noble, I fear that given the nature of the event coming up, all that'll come across here is the image of Bigger, the looming myth itself, and your celebratory rejection of it. Why don't you reread Baldwin's essay about the book and then try to think about what Baldwin has to say in relation to your own speech on Bigger Thomas?" I suggested. "He was an amazing public speaker, you know. One of those childhood preaching prodigies, famous as a kid speaking from pulpits in Harlem where his dad—also a rather brutal man it seems—was a minister. Anyway, you'll find all that in the book. I'll be back in next week. We'll have to see if the staff here will fax your next draft to campus."

"Will do, Dan," Noble said, gathering his papers and preparing to leave the room. He spent less time in the college room than many other of the most accomplished students, and his solitary times talking with Joseph and others went on elsewhere. He was cheerful and unperturbed, and I left with little hope that he'd rethink his speech or take a moment to read Baldwin on his own.

As I walked out of the room, I was confused, chastened, and disappointed. Before I could catch my breath, Salvio met me and led me into an empty classroom immediately across the narrow hallway. I was stunned by Joseph's message a few hours earlier that Salvio was another walk-out, and I wanted more information. I followed him in and we shut the door behind us.

I expected him to voice the same complaint as Malik, but he did not. For Salvio it had nothing to do with the rules governing the ceremony.

"I just don't want to go. I won't. I can't bear to do it in there."
I didn't understand. "In there? Where is 'there'?"

"In *there*. In the auditorium. My graduation should have been outside. On a lawn. All that this event in that auditorium means to me is that it's not on a lawn, with grass. It's about how much I've failed, and how much I've disappointed my family." He began to cry.

I looked into Salvio's boyish face and see, surprised again by the gray in his hair, the aging around his eyes and lips.

Incarceration is a long journey, terrible, in some small part, because it is marked by so few milestones. Its monotony, the threat that history, the experience of meaningful change over time, might be banished from one's life, may make up an important part of the punishment. It can amount to a kind of attenuated death sentence, measured out on a living and only partially aging being. At times, the prison has struck me as working like an eerie preservative, keeping long-term incarcerated people oddly youthful in appearance until, suddenly, years at a time descend and age them as if at once. The way they had to negotiate an endless labyrinth of rules and obstacles to balance the demands of both prison and college always stood for me as a sign of how much our students had to compromise to get and hold on to access, and how much we tacitly demanded of them every day. They, no doubt, needed no such reminder.

At home I reviewed my old copy of "Many Thousands Gone." I climbed the wobbly old ten-foot barn ladder that leans against the high wall of books behind my desk. Rereading Baldwin's opening lines, I balanced precariously on one of the rickety upper rungs.

> It is a sentimental error . . . to believe that the past is dead; it means nothing to say that it is all forgotten, that the Negro himself has forgotten it. It is not a question of memory. . . . The man does not remember the hand that struck him, the darkness that frightened him, as a child; nevertheless, the hand and the darkness remain

with him, indivisible from himself forever, part of the passion that drives him wherever he thinks to take flight.

Never, I thought, had such anger been fused into such poetry and such insight. My awe at Baldwin's achievement seemed only to grow as I matured, the more I saw of the world within which I worked. But what practical guidance could it offer to Nobe, or to me? Some of our students were black, many were white, Asian, or Latino; but all grappled with a version of the issues Baldwin had wrestled into genius, making his achievement part of the inheritance that came to all of us, as Americans. My mind turned again to Lloyd, to his fledgling and perhaps now aborted attempt to come to terms with Frederick Douglass, and with all that he had inherited from his talented and troubled family.

Two days later I received a fax of Noble's revisions. He had tweaked a couple of words in the text. He changed "rebellion" to "resistance." He added one line about Baldwin, quoting the young novelist as saying, "each of us has a story, and each story deserves to be told." My heart sank.

Noble was so close. But he brought a kind of reckless glee to his use of the iconography of Bigger on stage. Or perhaps the problem was that he was simply refusing to enact what I wanted him to, to read as I wanted him to read? No doubt he did not wish to engage with this text—any text, really—as we do when the college is working at its best. He wanted only to select, to sample, and with Baldwin he did so inaccurately, distorting the source and making it almost unrecognizable. On the perhaps petty level of institutional politics, in my mild paranoia I felt that the college's future was at stake. But along with that, I felt the liberal arts ethos was being cast rather publicly aside. In any case I was failing in my appointed tasks—both as a teacher, respectful of each student's wit and intelligence, and as a navigator of this treacherous piece of political theater.

Noble's quotation of Baldwin was a false one. Baldwin had never written that "each of us has a story to be told"—it just wasn't in there. It was a made-up quote and, worse—it was trivial and clichéd, in a way that cut against the very grain of Baldwin's essay, so concerned as it was with the representation of history and the creation of the symbols out of which we make our world.

At one level it was Noble's right to say whatever he wanted to about race, about prisons, about Bigger Thomas as an American figure—real or imagined—about the relationship of this image to the image of him and his classmates on the graduation stage. Was it not presumptuous in the extreme for me to intrude? Yet I also felt justified in thinking that the risk I perceived in Noble's choice of imagery was tied up with how little he was prepared to *do* college, to actually read and engage with Wright's Bigger, or Baldwin's Wright.

"I've been given a gun, and I intend to use it."

Back at Eastern, for one last try, Noble got us started.

"So, did you get my fax?" he asked.

"Yes," I nodded, holding up the curled sheets as the thermal paper decayed in my fingers.

He seemed genuinely interested in my reaction.

"I changed some pretty important words there. But not the heart of it."

"Yes."

"It's not 'rebellion' anymore—it's 'resistance.'"

"Yes, that's not insignificant. Look, Nobe, I think you're addressing something really important here, the audience's assumptions of who is here, about the images they hold when they walk through the gates and come into the auditorium, fascinated, to watch the graduation. But like I said last time, using Bigger Thomas to discuss all this is serious business," I said. "It requires—what to call it?—some care, some precision. And I really think that at times your

speech seems to do the opposite of what you want—to perpetuate the image, you know, the racial caricature, rather than to dispel it with the ceremony. Isn't this exactly Baldwin's concern with
Wright's novel? Would you mind reading this part aloud?"

I passed him the underlined copy of Baldwin that I had
brought from home.

> Below the surface of this novel there lies, as it seems to me, a con-
> tinuation, a complement of that monstrous legend it was written
> to destroy. . . .
>
> Bigger's tragedy is not that he is cold or black or hungry, not
> even that he is American, black; but that he has accepted a the-
> ology that denies him life, that he admits the possibility of his
> being sub-human and feels constrained, therefore, to battle for his
> humanity according to those brutal criteria bequeathed him at
> his birth. . . . The failure of the protest novel lies in its rejection
> of life, the human being, the denial of his beauty, dread, power, in
> its insistence that it is his categorization alone which is real and
> which cannot be transcended.

"That's impressive," Noble said. "But what else am I supposed
to do with it?"

"I don't know. Honestly, I'm not sure what to do with it."

"Yeah," he stopped, "I still don't really get the point. I'm
showing that the categorization is not real."

"Look, Nobe. If it's true that 'Bigger' remains today a phan-
tom that has somehow influenced your own fate and that of others here, then a more careful rhetorical combat needs to be waged
in order to challenge and remake it. And if not that, then maybe
only out of care for Baldwin? Why invoke Bigger at all?"

My voice trailed off and Noble looked at me blankly. "So, you
don't like my rhetoric, it makes you nervous and all. That's fine—I
toned it down for you a bit. Give me a break."

I sounded less like a teacher or comrade and more like a censor. Was that, in fact, what I had become? I tried to change my

tack. My voice turned more earnest—and less genuine. "This, you know, is to be BPI's first graduation. It's a kind of coming out for something that you and Max and I and all the others have taken years to build here inside. You know that the college has much less power than DOCS."

"Sure, man, I know that. Hey look, Dan, I never confuse you and Max with DOCS."

"I know that, Nobe, and it means a lot to me. And you know full well that DOCS reflects a lot more of, what shall we call it? The feelings of people at large." I paused for a second. "The sentiments of New York."

Noble laughed, "The People of the State of New York," he laughed, and I felt him coming back in closer to me. The less I cared about sorting out the Baldwin and the Bigger, the more easily the words came.

"And it's true, isn't it," I asked, "that our most important institutional ally is always just a misstep away from turning back into a dangerous antagonist? And we've never been on a bigger stage than we'll be on Saturday."

I was turning from careful if demanding teacher into a calculating administrator. This was an appeal to his own sense of power and ownership, in the hopes that he might be led to produce a text more favorable to what I took to be the college's immediate interests.

"There is a lot at stake here. Others will follow you into the college program, we hope, and their future opportunity is part of what you have the power to protect and to pass on. Consider that you are also an alumnus, a member of a small, prestigious college—one of the small group of pioneers, getting college back inside. When you speak from the podium next week, you can also see yourself as a representative of this college. At that moment you can act not only as inmate or student, but also on behalf of the college and the goal of college in prison throughout the system. A statesman."

Noble nodded, not speaking but leaning forward in the small chair. The image of the statesman, the man who tempered self-interest with the prudent calculation on behalf of the institution he led, seemed to resonate strongly with him. I knew at the time that my words felt condescending, but I was speaking to myself, as well, I thought. The text of Noble's speech, the horror of the novel's Bigger Thomas and the passionate tangle of Baldwin's critique, the graduate's wish to at once engage and remain aloof—all of this complexity faded under this new conceit that I found myself deploying.

With his threatening draft lying there before us on the table, I kept checking the clock on the wall behind him. I had one more speaker to meet, one more draft to read, before the module was ended and I was escorted out of the building, while Noble and the other students were sent back to their cells.

He too was glancing up at the clock, waiting for our encounter to end, waiting for the mandatory "go-back." Perhaps he was relieved to have a separation imposed on us.

I had precious few minutes left to meet with Joseph down the hall.

I reached out for Noble's hand.

"Noble. I mean this now. You can and will say whatever you want on Saturday. We can agree to disagree. If you want to take the risk, it's in no small part yours to run as well. This is a collective effort and always will be. But do think of what would be most effective—on behalf of the college of which you are now an alumnus."

Noble faced me in the doorway, exuding his usual sense of the playfulness and unflappable self-possession.

He offered me a parting word with a smile.

"I've been given a gun, Dan, and I intend to use it."

JOSEPH

With those words ringing in my ears, I walked down the whitewashed hall to meet Joseph. I had about an hour left, and I tried to keep the news about the defections of Calvin and Salvio out of my mind so I could focus on the person and the text before me.

Joseph was in another room across the hall, helping, as usual, a couple of other students with their homework. He was an institution-builder and would become a mentor to several cohorts of students who would later follow him into the college.

We decided to leave this busy room behind and instead took up a corner of the computer room across the hall. We sat down side-by-side in a pair of plastic and chrome chairs. These were identical to the ones I had sat in with Lloyd, two counties away and farther upstate, two distant years before.

Here was another person whose great creative and intellectual promise must have been obvious from a very early age. He was a student at the highly selective Bronx High School of Science at the time of his arrest. We shared a strong mutual affection and respect, muted by my professional reticence and his cautious irony. We shared a birthday and were nearly the same age. I had been his teacher for four years, and I looked forward to a time when his life would be different and we could more properly meet as the peers I already took us to be.

When Max was gathering the very first cohort of students for BPI, the department, in a genuine attempt to help assure its initial success, suggested that they be made up entirely of people with some previous college experience. Only five years before, there had been two or three different publicly funded college programs thriving at Eastern, and many of those students remained inside. The bulk of BPI's first cohort, then, had experience going to college inside. Yet Max had made two exceptions to the suggested rule, which had turned out to be very fortunate: Malik and Joseph.

When I later came on board, however, I had been warned by the education supervisor, the official staff hired to manage the GED and ABE and run the school area, that Joseph was more smart than shrewd, and deeply troubled. One of the semi-official pieces of advice they shared seemed a bit of correctional pedagogy or criminological psychology, namely, that this individual focused too intensely—a compulsive tendency characteristic of certain criminal types, of which he was a prototype. He thought too much about the prison—its workings, its tactics and effects—a paranoiac reaction, it was suggested, that afflicted certain bright but troubled inmates of the institution. In essence, we were advised not to waste a spot on such a type.

We *all* live in a perpetual dance of such figures: typologies, motifs, and pseudo-measurements; but people in institutions like prisons surely face the pressure of such symbols only more so.

Joseph joined the college and indeed focused on it with great intensity. In my first course offered in prison, Joseph had answered an exam question on Henry Clay's six-part Omnibus Bill of 1850 with such extraordinary detail that I had to consult the source books just to begin to grade it.

He was as precise in his handling of concepts as of facts. In another course we had read a piece by the historian Eric Foner that treated "freedom" as a key concept, a crucial but always changing and always contested part of the political tradition. Foner reviewed the shifting meanings of the term at crucial crossroads in American history. When the class had been asked to summarize the central idea of the article, Joseph had replied: "The main point is that freedom has a history. Excuse me, that's not quite right. It's that the *concept* of freedom has a history."

And from reading one or two short stories he had written for literature faculty, and some ethnographic work he had done in anthropology, I knew he also had a keen eye for the layers of meaning latent in the familiar details of everyday life. He loved abstractions but excelled at exploring them through closely observed details in mundane exchanges, spoken or otherwise.

Joseph could be intellectually vain but not at all arrogant: his well-earned self-regard had nothing to do with establishing superiority. He enjoyed giving and watching any good intellectual performance. Socially sensitive, he was a delicate participant in classrooms that were often full of less experienced or less capable students. At some point he had begun to mentor a number of other men in the college, who became his friends. He encouraged and tutored those not yet admitted but keen to get in. He often convinced those who felt themselves incapable to practice and apply. He spent many hours on his own work, but he could often be seen tutoring others in math or helping them revise a text of their own. I looked forward greatly to his draft, half-hoping his work would be a rhetorical island of both insight and prudence, on which the graduation could safely—and ambitiously—rely.

And then I read through the speech he handed me.

I was shocked, then disappointed, and then bored.

The speech was about transformation in prison, and it compared it to caterpillars as they turn from chrysalis to butterfly. In other words, it was just what most conventional audiences would expect—and hope—a student in prison to write. It was a flattering celebration of the rehabilitative effects of college in prison. Even worse, it was rambling and dull. Joseph's distinctive voice, intensely rational but elliptical and complex, was conspicuously absent.

Facing the same temptation to confront "the system," which Noble had embraced with such relish, Joseph had produced a mechanical exercise in flattery and accommodation. It read, if anything, like a formal submission for parole.

How was I to respond graciously to such a piece of writing?

I scanned it looking for a phrase with some promise, something from which he might push off and try again. And there, floating within the draft, was a passing reference to something called fêtes. These, he had written, were eighteenth-century American festivals he had studied in a class taught by Myra Armstead, a professor of history at Bard.

I tentatively suggested that the piece was a bit too predictable in its approach, with a few too many familiar images.

"I mean, really Joseph, is there any metaphor as endemic inside prisons as 'transformation'? You know better than I do how complicated it would be to really sort what goes on in here, in the college inside the prison, as far as cause and effect goes. In contrast to the official story of how this is supposed to work."

He nodded and fixed his eyes on me.

"So what do you think of beginning a revision with this stuff here?" I asked. "Page three—yes, here it is, yes, this reference to Myra's class. Inverted fêtes? That's quite interesting."

There was a pause, as he looked at me, and I detected a slight smile on his lips. Yet he said nothing, waiting.

"It's the one thing in your current draft that is concrete—I mean that comes specifically from your own experience with the college. You *suggest* that it's relevant to the graduation ceremony but you don't say why or how. I haven't read the book. Tell me— what are 'perpetual fêtes' and what do they have to do with the graduation?"

Joseph's gaze was unreadable behind his prison-issue glasses.

Finally he said quite matter-of-factly: "I wrote another speech. But I put it aside." Pointing to the draft I held in my hand, he said, "This was my alternative. I thought it might be considered more. . . . appropriate."

I looked back at him, trying to mirror his inscrutable face although that was not my usual style. More often than not, I enjoyed the luxury of frankness.

"Considered more appropriate by whom? By me?"

He shrugged and said nothing.

He must have spoken with Noble. Perhaps word of my overly coercive approach to the Bigger idea had affected him?

And then I remembered something else long-forgotten. Joseph had been chosen once already by his classmates to be the speaker—in a small certificate ceremony—like the ones in which Lloyd and the other students at Greene had taken such pride. A less elaborate affair, it had marked the successful completion of our first tentative semesters inside. And yes, it had come with a makeshift certificate.

On that earlier occasion, before a small audience of college faculty and fellow prison inmates, Joseph had read a speech that was banal and predictable, a text cushioned—and muffled—by cliché. Then, afterward, I had been told regretfully by other students that he had read to them a draft of his speech in a private session a day or so beforehand, and during that earlier private reading of his full speech, he, and a number of them as well, had wept. At the last minute, before the little ceremony years before, he had decided to replace his beautifully crafted speech with one largely improvised: safe, and insipid.

How could I have forgotten this back-story? Our most promising speaker for Saturday had faced a similar if much less challenging moment before and had silenced himself.

"Joseph," I said, "I'm here to worry about the best interests of the college. I'm looking out for us—you know, the whole dynamic between the ceremony, the college, the prison, whatever. So, at least for a moment, why don't you let *me* worry about what's appropriate? Share with me, here, the speech you really want to give. The one you *really* like."

He didn't miss a beat.

"Do you remember," he asked, "the incident with Mr Schmidt?"

Indeed I did. It had been one of those charged moments that flare up in the prison day like a little brushfire. Most of them go out; some of them blow up. They are rarely discussed and typically slip into oblivion. They might show up in a journal, or a letter home; or, much later on, in a prison memoir, a short story, or an incident report.

For a teacher coming and going, such flare-ups occur while being processed by security staff at the gate, or in the corridors going to and from the school at the prison's interior, in the moments where one finds oneself in spontaneous encounters outside of class with prison staff, students, or other inmates.

I recalled this incident: A couple of months earlier, time had run out on a class I was teaching and we were moving from the classroom to the college's general-purpose library across the hall. The education supervisor's office was the room next door. Several students and I were continuing the conversation, running beyond the allotted time and outside of the assigned space. We were milling about at the threshold between the prison hallway and the college classroom. Fraternizing in the halls was against the prison rules.

In passing, Mr Schmidt was thus exposed to something from which he was usually insulated: the scene of our students of our students—his inmates—talking skillfully and passionately with a college professor about the course.

"What is *this*," he had sneered jovially, "the new street corner?"

The students had fallen silent.

This petty affront, unlike countless others, was played out in front of me, a figure from the "other world" of the college that these men occupied with us, adjacent to but a fragile world away from Mr Schmidt's prison-school territory. The students could not reply, no matter what the tone, without risking punishment. This silencing, a part of their daily lives, was rarely acted out in front of visiting faculty. Indeed, the college's life was woven out of freedoms of thought and speech and self-presentation made more acute by their contrast with the *habitus* of the surrounding institution. In the temporary space of the college, norms of discipline persist with great intensity, but are dislocated and rearranged. It's no utopia, but it certainly resonates with the idea of one, conjured by the college, invented by its students, and intensified by the contrast with the prison.

Mr Schmidt apparently thought he was being friendly.

Without thinking and responding in the same jovial tone, I called back quickly, "*No*, not the new street corner. It's the new agora."

AFTER RECALLING THIS incident, I responded, "Yes, Joseph, I remember the exchange."

"Well, that's what I wrote about for my talk. I was interested in what he said, of course, about 'What is this, the new street corner?' and I was also interested in your answer, 'No, the new *agora*.' At first, I liked your answer of course. I mean, I knew what he was getting at, and the whole moment there at the threshold of class, spilling into the hall where we're not supposed to be hanging out together. And I knew what *you* were getting at too when you answered back. But later I thought to myself, *wait a minute*, this is two white men, both in positions of authority, and what they're doing is talking about *us*, about me and the other students, and *they're* naming *us*, describing what *we* do, deciding on terms, like *agora*, which is 'good' and *street corner*, which is 'bad.' So I wrote this draft, the one I'm *not* going to show you," his eyes sparkled, "about you and Mr Schmidt naming us, and characterizing what we do when we do our work in the college. And I wrote about the street corner, and you know."

Joseph paused here for a moment before resuming.

"I really miss my old neighborhood, I *miss* the Bronx and I miss the street corner. When we're here—in the college, studying—you know what that is for me? That's the closest I can get now back to that old feeling, to that street corner, to what was best about my life back home. And I pictured one of these teachers driving through my old neighborhood, in their car, looking through their moving window with the doors locked, seeing a bunch of guys, who look like us, who look like me, standing around on the corner, and this person would look at us, and say, 'See that? They're probably involved in a transaction.'"

He paused again.

"And he'd be right. We almost certainly would be—involved in a transaction."

I could hardly contain my delight. Yes, I did wince a bit, knowing that Mr Schmidt and I were both "one of these teachers" driving along the boulevard with the windows up, the car doors locked, looking and naming. But I was impressed by how he thought and I was entertained by how he spoke.

Joseph continued, "We'd be talking amongst ourselves, a lot like we were doing when we were talking about your class, at the doorway of that room there, and in real, you know, communication between people. *That's* a transaction. And who knows what is, and is not, illicit?"

For Joseph, his delight in the college, his flourishing in increasingly advanced studies, from social theory to calculus, was entirely of a piece with his life before, as a teenager in the Bronx. The pursuit of every form of learning the college could offer him only further dignified and reciprocated the modes of living and learning he had always known back home. Of course, his act of appropriating was a critique and a tribute both. I loved his sense of humor. But above all, perhaps, I was flattered that he shared it with me in this way, his analysis of me and my position, mine and Mr Schmidt's, in the kind of free exchange among equals that showed me, in his inimitable style, the utopia that the college could be, because people like Joseph brought it into being in thoughtful words and actions.

"I see why you find this a bit confrontational," I said, smiling. "But in my opinion—well, it couldn't be *more* appropriate for graduation. I love it." Then I added: "And in this version, Joseph, the one you're patting in your breast pocket but won't show me— do the fêtes still come into play?"

He frowned. "Do you think *that* still fits?" he asked.

"I don't know. It could, I suppose. You know, one of my many problems as a writer is that I tend to think almost *anything* of interest can fit, if you connect the dots, compose it right. That idea from Myra's class—the inverted fêtes—that was the glimmer in your redacted version, the speech you offered for popular consumption—or for my official scrutiny—" I smiled "—it might very well fit. Commencement and inverted fêtes? Something tells me you can work whatever it is you're thinking about that material back into your real speech."

He nodded distractedly, already mulling the puzzle over.

I left the room, stinging a bit from Joseph's analysis of the exchange between me and Mr Schmidt, but brimming with pleasure at this great speech he had in the works. And after the remorse I felt at trying to coax Noble *out* of giving the speech he wanted, I felt some redeeming pride that Joseph could turn his critical gaze onto me with confidence in my professionalism, and maybe also, in my friendship. He had tested me—with his fake draft, his safe draft—and I hoped that, in his eyes, I had passed.

As I made my way down the warren of hallways and corners and stairwells, and along the long, county road back to campus, it seemed that the circuitous exchange with Joseph had captured almost everything that the college, and what we were doing together at Eastern, were about. And yes, crossing the bridge over the Hudson River en route to campus, I knew that Joseph's first draft was a test, a feint, to see how I would respond to its clichés and its avoidance of anything difficult. That explained his odd, self-satisfied smile when I suggested that his first draft was lousy.

There was no time for another meeting, and Joseph would decide what speech to give.

Of course, if enough graduates refused even to attend, the speeches would end up a sideshow when they should have been the main event. Would Malik, Calvin, and Salvio really boycott? If that happened, the entire day would be a disaster. And would Noble make use of his rhetorical "gun," as he had called it? The college—along with its allies in the administration—would appear sloppy, unprofessional, "out of control." The students ungrateful, stubborn, unrepentant. Two weeks earlier I had fancied myself the skillful stage manager of an elaborate piece of politically charged institutional theater. Now I was nearly exhausted, and all I had learned was just how little control I had over the program I had helped to run for so long.

The night before commencement, Max and I were reviewing the status quo, discussing Malik, Salvio, and the others. We still had no idea who would show up. I said, "Max, it's terribly hard for them, this graduation. And that's a shock to me. It shouldn't be. But it has been."

Max replied, "Yeah, that's right. But how else can you do this work—without shutting your eyes to that, without forgetting that?"

Max said he'd rather wait outside the building until it was all over, rather than having to host the myriad guests in the glare both on and off the stage. We had worked for this for so long—especially Max—yet it seemed neither of us could wait until this weekend was over.

Graduation Day

For one afternoon everybody stood in the same line. The guests' arrival deadline was 9:30 that morning. It would take at least two hours for the prison to sort the 300 visitors who had driven up to attend BPI's first graduation.

Most of the audience was coming from New York City. Many had been up in the predawn darkness readying themselves. People of every ethnicity, every finely graded New York social class and background became part of a single, snake-like line winding through the prison lobby. The line at security formed a slow-moving romería of investors from Manhattan and bodega keepers from the boroughs, of renowned academics and taxi drivers, of white-shoe lawyers and off-duty cops. The wealthy guests knew that the city's affluent enclaves were policed on their behalf, and that the prison was part of the same power that protected them discreetly where they lived, worked, and traveled. For others, the trip through prison security to visit a loved one was all too familiar.

Guests who had never entered the prison before ran up against the inconveniences of its protocol. Some had neglected to bring their licenses; others had forgotten to leave their cellphones and pagers in the car. High-end electronics were a social equalizer—for rich or poor, everybody carried the same gadgets. Likewise, the security processes were a good example of "democratizing down," of equalizing people through a shared experience of potentially humiliating compliance. The forgetful had to run back into the cold, leaving their overcoats awkwardly in the arms of the stranger standing next to them in line, returning huffing and flustered, their breath visible in the frosty air. Most institutions sort social groups and thus hide the divisions among us, keeping them out of sight; the line at Eastern made the gulfs obvious, by bringing us all together.

I made my way back deeper into the prison and its central auditorium. My gaze rapidly scanned the crowd gathering in the dim, cavernous hall. The din of a dozen fans bolted into the vaulted ceiling sixty feet above, reverberated off the concrete walls and the hundred rows of bolted plastic chairs.

Guests moved through the room, speaking quietly among themselves or chatting with exaggerated deference to the occasional graduate. They found places to sit, choosing between proximity to the bulking proscenium or the sea of inmates, made up largely of guests from "general population," who sat in the back rows of the auditorium marked off with yellow tape.

All the graduates wore conventional black graduation robes, which hid the prison greens beneath except at the very bottom where the green peeked out beneath the hem.

Nervously I sought word of our status quo.

"How many speakers do we have today, Joseph?"

He paused, deadpan.

"Four," he said, and allowed a smile to break out.

So among the speakers, at least, the prospect of a graduate boycotting had been avoided.

"And how many refusals overall?"

"Just Malik," he answered.

"And Salvio?"

"He'll be here. But he told his family not to come."

All the guests were seated. In the front rows were arrayed the graduates themselves, all in black caps and gowns. Up on stage were the faculty, like tropical birds, in their honorific robes, along with the college president, the trustees, the commissioner of the prison system, the superintendent, myself, and Max. The brass quartet in their tuxedos began to play Bard's signature commencement piece, the leitmotif that conjured up memories of all Bard graduations in all parts of the world, Brahms's *Variations on a Theme by Haydn*.

The dozen graduates were called up to the stage in succession by the dean, and each received his diploma from the president. Malik's name was called too, appended with the phrase, especially uncanny here, "in absentia." He was with his own guests who had come to Eastern that day, off at the other end of the facility, in the visiting room. All the others came and "walked," including Salvio. He stood alone both before and after the procession, the only graduate with no one in attendance on his behalf.

Noble began his speech. "In the words of James Baldwin, 'Each of us has a story, and each story deserves to be told.'" Fortunately, it wasn't "Each of us here is Bigger Thomas." But still my heart sank.

He continued, in sonorous tones and smooth, familiar, reassuring cadences. "We on this stage, stand before you today to illustrate the miracle of the chrysalis, the metamorphosis of life as it matures and develops. . . . ." He did not "use the gun" that he had been given, and for that I was grateful. Instead, it sounded like Joseph's discarded text, or some variation on it. He neither engaged the Baldwin nor hammered out a vision of his own argument about what was wrong with the "image" of men of prison and what was at stake in how they were fashioning a new image to project from the stage that day. He did not take up Baldwin's challenge to involve himself in "the force of life and legend" that is consolidated in terms that adhered to them like "convict" or "inmate."

Instead, Noble pointed to himself and his fellow graduates as proof that change can happen, and that good men can grow out of a bad past. He invoked the cocoon, which after mysterious ages of gestation gives forth the butterfly.

I felt at the time that Noble was giving a speech he didn't believe in, and which expressed little or nothing of what he had wanted to say about the achievements of himself and his fellow graduates. He took up the role of the dutiful inmate, and worse, of the obedient student. He had accepted my strategic plea to become a statesman of the college, to defend its project, but in doing so he had compromised his instincts and the truth as he felt it. As I listened to the story of the chrysalis and the butterfly, I deeply regretted the form of his capitulation, and my role in it. It was an act of generosity toward the college, as I had presented its needs, but also an abandonment of the college's deeper purpose and values. I wanted to have it both ways. This was his gift to me, and, in my heart, ungenerously, I wanted to spurn it.

Afterward, many people said they loved the speech, thought it expressed so much, and found it, above all, inspirational.

And then it was time for the final speech—which was, for me, a revelation.

Joseph was called to the stage and began to straighten himself at the podium.

As an expectant silence settled over the auditorium, he drew a pair of glasses from a breast pocket beneath his robes and slowly put them on. He declared his wish to share with the audience an example of the kind of topic that, as he put it, "we studied here at Eastern with Bard."

With his characteristic attention to detail, he was choosing not to echo our habit of referring to everything that went on there simply as "Bard": the fiction that suffused the best of our efforts. But neither would he reject that conceit, reducing the place he evoked to "Eastern," to the prison alone. He would have his own way of characterizing the balance between these institutions, between which he had lived for the past several years, en route to his degree.

"The topic I've chosen to discuss with you today," Joseph continued, "concerns public ceremonies from the early nineteenth century called 'inverted fêtes.' The topic comes from David Waldstreicher's *In the Midst of Perpetual Fêtes* and was introduced to us by the venerable Dr Myra Armstead, chair of Bard's History Department, in her course entitled 'Making National Citizens.'"

His style was theatrical, and he embellished his delivery by playfully imitating the academic mannerisms of professors at the podium. But this mild satire was done with a kind of lighthearted ease that seemed more affectionate than critical. This only became more clear as he continued, for it was soon evident that his speech was devoted, in part, to a nuanced exploration of the content of one of his favorite classes. He was teasing the faculty a bit, but also paying tribute to them by doing so well, and with great care and seriousness, what he knew they loved most, and what he had enjoyed so deeply in their company over the preceding years.

These festivals, he explained, were historical events in early America; they were days of unique celebration in nineteenth-century rural society. During these "fêtes," the normal social hierarchies were "inverted." Enslaved laborers were allowed to dress up and behave like their social superiors, while those same masters "condescended" to come down off their horses and out of their formal garb to mingle, drink, and dance among the commoners.

He looked out over the audience as he continued, telling how these festivals of inversion provided a relief from slavery's extreme hierarchy in the midst of Jacksonian America. These risky social theatricals, he suggested, had served both to unsettle and sustain the system as it was.

"We here at Eastern," he said, "often wonder how our counterparts on the main campus respond to the same courses offered here that they have taken on campus. Professor Armstead is devoted to teaching exactly the same things, in the same way, that she does on the 'main campus'—but she too is interested in the differences that arise from our different circumstances."

Joseph said that Dr Armstead found conventional students back on the main campus were at first confused by the idea of perpetual fêtes. But once they understood it, they didn't see why it was interesting. What had any of this to do with helping historians understand antebellum America?

"We here at Eastern, however," he pointed out to his graduation audience, "took to the idea of these fêtes at once. We found it insightful and fascinating about life under slavery in an otherwise increasingly democratic America. It seemed to come naturally to us, for whatever reason."

I marveled at the speech and did my best to keep up with its many frames and story lines. Joseph had begun with this odd imitation of his own professors (putting on the glasses, straightening himself up on stage)—a bit of mockery—appropriate to an inverted fête, perhaps. He played up the physical side of the comedy in his performance, slowly putting on his reading glasses, gazing out confidently at his audience, and taking ostentatious command of the podium. He was making fun of his professors' academic performances, and of his own role in addressing the graduation audience, managing with irony the various roles he was called upon to play, both those he desired and those imposed upon him. He engaged his audience in the details of study—but also with the meaning of the encounter between the college and the prison, and the meaning of the ceremony that day. He invoked for his audience the always implicit juxtaposition between the two different, concurrent Bard worlds—the one on the main campus and the one inside the prison. He introduced the idea of inverted fêtes, as if it were simply one example of the sorts of things they might study in an American history class—but of course, he was suggesting that this idea shed light not only on how contemporary American history is written, but also about what we were all taking part in that day at Eastern.

Then he made the transition into his story of the hallway scene, of the two men self-consciously occupying their positions of authority—an unnamed college administrator, and an unnamed prison education official, as they had jockeyed in front of "their" students, competing to see who would successfully define the men ("scholars" versus "offenders") and, by extension, the status of conversation that had spilled out of the classroom that day and into the prison hallway.

Noble's speech about the chrysalis and the transformative power of education in prison was a great success. The audience loved it—they applauded and cheered during its delivery, and afterward celebrated how moving it was, how much it revealed about what had brought us all together. By comparison, Joseph's speech was less successful with the audience. Most of the people I heard discussing it afterward had not been able to follow it, found it too convoluted or challenging, and had decided to tune it out after the first few minutes. Others had been distracted by the physicality of his humor, his almost burlesque parody of academic manners. Few seemed to have been interested in following along with his intellectual allegory and its multiple frame narratives, which were, admittedly—like the prison, and like the college within it—myriad and challenging. A few of us loved it, and several thought it the best commencement address they'd ever heard. But most were indifferent, or preoccupied, and somewhat disturbed by his odd, even ironic, delivery.

Following these and the other two speeches, the audience cheered. Graduates advanced to the podium as the dean read their names, calling them back to the stage one by one. Walking up the several steps, they advanced to receive a diploma from the hands of the president. In a fluid instant, the one handed the scroll into the outstretched hand of the other, right to left, as simultaneously they shook hands and turned to face the professional photographer who was in the shadows below the proscenium. I wondered at the easy way all of these minute physical transactions transpired, unrehearsed. For the graduates, each was the first occasion of a lifetime; for the president of the college, it was a choreographed ritual executed—and directed—with effortless familiarity. It all came off smoothly.

When the diplomas were handed out, we all gathered for lunch in the inmate mess hall, a cavernous, gymnasium-like room. Freed from the auditorium's bolted chairs and the yellow police tape that had cordoned off the zone of seating, graduates and family and college guests mingled freely.

Noble came up to me, smiling and exuberant, flush with the pride of his personal success and the public culmination of the college's years of effort. He took my hand and spoke to me of how important I had been to him—as a teacher, and as a person.

"I'm giving you love, Karpowitz. That's what we call this!" and squeezed my hand harder. He was elated, and I felt relief in his recognition, pleased at how satisfied he was with how the day had gone.

"It's mutual," I said, swept up in his enthusiasm and everyone's shared sense of triumph.

I sought out the parents of those graduates to whom the college would always be indebted, as they had done so much to build the college at Eastern.

Yet as I spoke to Joseph's stern-faced father, my words fell flat. I could read nothing on the face of this man whose adult son had been my student in prison and had become, as much as the circumstances and our respective personalities seemed to permit, an intellectual companion and professional friend. I was his son's age, and my own father and mother were there that day, too. I told him that his son was not only a brilliant student, but also that the college owed him a debt of gratitude—for he had been a mentor to others and had often guided us in our work.

The man watched me, expressionless.

"He has built something precious here under difficult circumstances. Something that will last and be of great service to those who come after him. We're very proud of him."

The father nodded, and that was all.

As the meal ended, our fête dissolved. The men who had graduated and spent the day in the glow of the college went back to being prisoners. They removed their black robes and assumed the college greens. As if by osmosis, they were slowly sorted out of the mingling crowd of visitors and assembled on the farthest side of the mess hall. There, under the gaze of the line of officers that had materialized, they were formed into a line to be counted, recorded, and led out through the doors. The guests waited and watched, left with only each other to talk to, the vastness of the building around them, the men who had brought them together, gone. The commencement was over.

Driving home, I was exhausted and high, en route to an evening of eating and drinking with colleagues and friends, the BPI family, in a farmhouse near campus. As always, the joy was compromised with sorrow. This first great milestone in our work, as would so often be the case, took place in the shadow of an even greater waste that nothing in our work could ameliorate.

Joseph had begun by censoring himself and proceeded to achieve a remarkably full expression, which I could both learn from and admire. Noble's trajectory was the inverse: he had begun with exuberant self-assertion, flawed I felt, but not because he had chosen the wrong target. Convinced to "play the game," but not to fully culminate the work—he had ended up in cliché, presented to me as a gift that I had, perhaps, appeared to be asking for. It was equally possible that my exaggerated investment in the outcome had made it harder for me to read his original intentions and to clarify my own.

Years since, I have gone back to both speeches, looking through the fragments of student drafts that I have in files and notebooks.

In hindsight, Noble's original speech appears not nearly as incendiary as it struck me at the time. No longer overshadowed by my exaggerated fear of his invoking Bigger Thomas from the stage, or my frustration with his refusal to read or think about Baldwin, one line of his draft, the audience never had the chance to hear, stands out to me. Noble had written that the graduation was the celebration of "a movement, a work in process, whose aim is to ensure that no story is killed before it has the chance to announce itself."

Joseph had begun by concealing what he truly thought and felt. Perhaps he was protecting his own feelings, or testing me, or trying to avoid challenging his audience. For Joseph was as suspicious of the optics of the stage as we was of the motives of its managers. In the end, however, he had mastered a distinctive art—the art of writing and speaking freely in confinement. His speech was neither a submission nor a rebellion, and it brought home Osiatynski's lessons about our constitutional ideal. It was indeed a public text and a significant political achievement, written and delivered in prison. He had calibrated it to protect himself, his classmates, and the vulnerable college he himself had worked so hard to build. Yet at the same time he had directed the force of his intellect onto the contemporary prison and how much its meaning today resonates with the deepest parts of our historical legacy, of a past which continues to divide us and bind us together. Most remarkably, perhaps, he had fashioned a commentary on the college's wish to stamp his and the others' achievements in its own image, through the peculiar spectacle that they had all participated in that day. He did this in a way that truly was a celebration and a tribute. But it also revealed something broader, namely how, in the words of Craig Wilder, the American historian and a frequent BPI professor, "the whole enterprise has a certain cruelty embedded in it, boundaries seen and unseen, impossible expectations and demands, embarrassing roles that must be played," culminating in a "celebration that is also, oddly, a trial."

In May 2014, four years after completing his eighteen-year prison sentence, Joseph graduated with a master's degree in epidemiology from Columbia University. Shortly after his first graduation at home, held on Columbia's main campus, I wrote and asked him to tell me what he remembered about the speech he had given ten years before, at BPI's first graduation. Here is his reply, in full:

> Good morning DK. Inverted fêtes came from Dr Armstead's class, Making National Citizens. In my mind, the inverted fêtes were a moment when the powerful provided a space for slaves to create a governmental structure. The slaves were being mocked through this gesture, which also served an important function for the powerful to allow the "powerless" to let off steam. The slaves mocked the power structure and had "gub'nor 'lections" and cake walks. But then the "gub'nors" became figures that the powerful had to negotiate with. As the day wound down the slaves turned power back over to the masters, but among the masters there was always the fear that this would not happen. So, I guess, a part of my message was that students did not have to turn power back over when the celebration/graduation ended. That, if we had to, we could continue to maintain the powerful meaning of the space of prison and the college in the prison. That we could get past mocking a graduation as self-determining men, and feeling mocked ourselves—not simply inverting power but assuming it.

CHAPTER 5

Replication and Conclusions

COLLEGE, PRISON, AND INEQUALITY IN AMERICA

COLLEGE IN PRISON sits at the intersection between two distinctly American institutions: the undergraduate college and the state penitentiary. Since well before the nation's founding, the American college has been an institution of wealth and privilege that eventually justified itself as a private institution dedicated to the public interest. All began as training schools for ministers, but some included the seeds of what became an ever-evolving liberal arts curriculum that embodied a vision of spiritual emancipation. At the same time, we know that the accumulated capital on which these colleges were all built, and their crucial role in shaping thought about the concept of "race," were entwined with the institutions and justifications of slavery as well as, eventually, of emancipation. The penitentiary, in contrast to America's oldest private educational legacies, has always been a creature of the state, and from the outset showcased its awesome concentration of public power. It too was an institution born of the early United States, and while it embodied a revolutionary optimism in the public's ability to coercively reform the individual, it was also always steeped in state violence and, often, symbols as well as practices rooted in slavery. If part of the penitentiary was rooted in a reformist zeal of liberal emancipation, celebrating individual agency, the context in which it grew easily shaped it into a cult of secular salvation based on punitive labor and spiritual conformity. Both the college and the prison emerged at the dawn of American society and, in each successive generation, have helped define the democracy's enduring conflicts over public and private power, the belief in change, and inequality.

Today, both the college and the prison remain characteristic institutions whose disproportionate influence looms large over American society. The private liberal arts college enrolls only about 1 percent of American college students, but it retains its disproportionate role in the selection and formation of governing elites. Questions of access, vision, and equality continue to be central to the improvement of such colleges, as they do for the far more vast networks of the country's public colleges and universities. The prison has become, perhaps more than ever before, a powerful instrument in the reproduction of inequality, whether understood as a measure of race, or class, or, most appropriately, both. College remains a formative instrument in the production of middle- and upper-class status. Prison has become central to what many analysts refer to as our "carceral state," and the experience of it has become epidemic for poorer Americans, especially those without a college degree. Even worse, it is what the sociologist Bruce Western calls a "modal" experience in the life-course of many African American men.

Both the college and the prison remain sites where we imagine and construct divergent models of democratic selves. This has profound consequences for the society as a whole and for the futures of the individuals, networks, and indeed communities that pass through them. Regardless of whether or not we have "college in prison," the two institutions share parallel roles in the reproduction of American privilege and inequality. Indeed, the dynamics of contemporary American inequality most closely track two divergent life-paths: through college on the one hand, prison on the other.

A Case for College in Prison

At the beginning of the book, conflicting voices laid out some of the arguments against college in prison. These included the claim that, given the severity and inequities of American mass incarceration, this sort of intervention does far too little. It affects the lives of only a handful of people in prison when the entire system needs radical reform or, as some argue, outright abolition. For other critics, however, the presence of college in prison does too much, making it seem as if there is something morally or politically wrong with punishment, as if individuals are not rightly held culpable for their own actions.

I have some sympathy with the first of these criticisms. But I feel that a great deal can and must be done to assure the dignity and future prospects of people currently incarcerated, even while we commit to major and systematic reductions in the overuse of prison. Dignified educational opportunity that prepares individuals today for a life beyond prison is at the very least an urgent if temporary measure, en route to changes that may someday be far more profound.

By way of conclusion, I offer three broad arguments on behalf of college in prison. The first, closest to my heart, is moralistic, and it suggests the place that I think this work has in a kind of social theory of punishment. It leads directly into the second, a more political view, namely that how the state handles criminal justice makes us who we are. Both of these closely related arguments might serve as an alternative to, or a bridge between, conventional thinking on the "right" and "left." The third argument, refreshingly, has nothing to do with crime, punishment, or even prisons. Surprisingly perhaps, it is the one closest to the founding vision of BPI itself.

A Moral Argument

One contemporary conservative complaint is that college in prison undermines our moral clarity. On the contrary, however, college in prison is one way to make the meaning and experience of criminal accountability a more honest expression of our avowed love of freedom. Our best justifications for much criminal and civil law rest on the belief that free people can and must be held morally accountable for their actions. If this is so, then our systems of accountability—be they punitive, rehabilitative, restorative, or restitutive (based on financial compensation rather than punishment)—should strengthen both agency and dignity. But prisons, of course, tend to degrade human integrity and cripple personal agency. Institutions predicated on dignity and the respect for free choice must cultivate these very capacities. Otherwise, they become a mockery, and they reveal the hypocrisy of the stated values. This line of thought would lead to recognizing that punishment is by no means the only or best mechanism for the pursuit of moral accountability. In a social reality marked by strong class and racial inequality, the moral justifications of prison are weakened to the point of collapse.

Finally, our rhetoric too often uses the fact of individual moral responsibility to absolve the public of its own shared, political responsibility for structural injustice. Instead of engaging both at once, the community in flight from its collective duties turns the individual into the scapegoat for the group. In no sense can college in prison resolve this tension, but it does live on the fault line of these contradictions, and is thus the sort of action that helps make our public institutions, like prisons, ethically worthy of the republic they sustain.

A Political Argument

The second argument is more frankly political and holds that things like college in prison express, above all, the character of a political order. One's attitudes toward punishment reflect one's attitudes toward government itself—its power, its aspirations, its limits. The sociologist David Garland has characterized our era's "culture of control" as a desperate effort by governments, weakened by global economic forces and ideological attack, to engage in the "acting out" of power: the state's exaggerated, last-ditch attempt to show that it has potency amid the predominant fear that it is, on the contrary, losing strength.

For those who wish to go down an alternative path, a relevant view may have been expressed best by Winston Churchill, the most famous twentieth-century advocate of "one-nation Conservatism." Due to the odd connections and marked differences between British political traditions and our own, his words might serve as a bridge between progressive and conservative thinking on this topic in America. His remarks, given as Home Secretary speaking to the House of Commons on July 20, 1910, deserve to be quoted in full:

> The mood and temper of the public in regard to the treatment of crime and criminals is one of the most unfailing tests of the civilization of any country. A calm and dispassionate recognition of the rights of the accused against the state and even of convicted criminals against the state . . . tireless efforts towards the discovery of curative and regenerating processes and an unfaltering faith that there is a treasure, if only you can find it in the heart of every person—these are the symbols which in the treatment of crime and criminals mark and measure the stored up strength of a nation, and are the sign and proof of the living virtue in it.

Here is a vision that embraces college in prison not only as an intervention in the fate of individual citizens, but also as a constitutive expression of cultural power itself, as a defining act of government. This is close in spirit to what I meant earlier in the book, when I suggested that college in prison should be conceived less about how people in prison might change and more about how we, as a society increasingly defined by the scope and quality of our prisons, might change ourselves.

I think this way of looking at the problem may resonate most strongly with the crucial allies of BPI in the public sector, including prison officials, who work to advance this work in states across the country. The daily compulsion of their jobs and our political era require them to manage regimes of ever-increasing scarcity and deprivation for humane activities like education (in and out of prison). And most of the time, like other public officials in our day and age, they are compelled to defend and explain their decisions through entirely pragmatic and narrowly budgetary terms. This of course reflects a general degradation of our political culture and a sclerosis of our public policy. But I sense that the political vision that leads such officials to embrace opportunities like those presented by BPI is one that resonates with the sense of optimism and confidence in the words quoted above.

Arguments drawn from the narrower realm of "policy" are, of course, available, and are often quite persuasive. But they might be more effective, and more honest, if they were situated within the larger sorts of arguments I offer here. For many years, indeed for decades, the "costs and benefits" of providing access to college-level education in prison have been measured and studied. And they have inevitably produced compelling results, based in part on the argument that college in prison correlates with dramatically lowered rates of recidivism. After fifteen years, for example, BPI's rate of recidivism is about 4 percent among all of those who have participated, and close to 2 percent for those who have completed a degree. The comparable base-line rate of recidivism in New York ranges around 40 percent.

Yet all of this was true in the 1990s, when Congress withdrew Pell eligibility from people in prison. Despite the fact that such interventions appeared to be the most sensible piece of in-prison programming and cost next to nothing, they were defunded. This was done, as I have noted earlier, over the objections of the people who actually run the prisons. But the analysis of costs and benefits had no impact whatsoever on Congress's decision, at once theatrical and devastating, to destroy such programs. Recent studies, such as the one produced by the Rand Corporation in 2013, confirm earlier research. They serve as rhetorical support for renewed efforts by state officials and private foundations to rebuild post-secondary educational opportunity as one feature of American correctional policy. Such efforts will be more honest, and perhaps more successful, if the reasons for doing them are articulated in a broader and more courageous vision of who we want to be.

BPI AND AMERICAN HIGHER EDUCATION

My final argument on behalf of BPI and college in prison is about American higher education. It has nothing at all to do with crime or punishment. It is this far broader view that is closest, I think, to the heart of Max Kenner, who founded BPI, and of Ellen Lagemann, the historian of education who is a close, and our most senior colleague, and who herself has recently written a book devoted to this topic.

Higher education has in the past managed to be both excellent and inclusive, and it can be so again. According to a recent report from the White House, twenty-five years ago the United States ranked first in the developed world on the portion of young adults who had earned a four-year degree. Today we are twelfth. Indeed, the advent of mass incarceration has coincided with the dramatic constriction of funding for higher education and the increasingly narrow range of Americans who can afford it. As noted earlier, many have argued that there is a causal, and not merely indirect and structural, connection between these two phenomena, as public expenditures appear to have been shifted away from investments in higher education and into spending on prisons and other forms of carceral control.

With the dismantling of affirmative action across the country, colleges and universities are experimenting with new ways to create broader opportunity, but they are not doing enough, especially at our most prestigious schools. The story of increased indebtedness among students and their families is well known, as are the struggles—and conflicting, nearly impossible mandates—imposed upon our community colleges, even while public funding for them is systematically undermined.

BPI is perhaps best understood as one of the bright spots in American higher education, as private and public university systems, along with parents and students, seek new ways to achieve what is called "inclusive excellence." BPI is an example of how we can address what the White House, in its Call to Action on College Opportunity, has joined in identifying as core strategic goals. These include overcoming "academic undermatch," in which our best but poorest students never connect to a school that can live up to their abilities; and aggressively restructuring what are unfortunately called, in the language of investment banking, the "returns to selectivity"—the extreme and growing inequality of resources available to students in "selective" as opposed to "more open" colleges, and the tremendous social, economic, and political advantages that accrue to students who graduate from the more selective and resource-rich institutions. To my mind, this calls for far greater support, and perhaps higher ambitions, for our more open institutions, but also far more imaginative and courageous efforts on the part of our more selective ones.

The fact that BPI and its students have achieved such successes in intellectual ambition and integrity, in academic achievement, and in professional life, is a testament both to their strengths and to the resilience of liberal arts learning. It is also a testament to the extraordinary ability of unconventional students, whom educational systems have long failed, to cultivate rigorous skills and, above all, a profound sense of dignity and purpose. It is true, as the MIT historian and BPI professor Craig Wilder has said, that there is a way out of our failed policies of mass incarceration, if only we have the courage to take it. It is also true that BPI is, most broadly understood, a model for how our colleges and universities, in partnership with the extraordinary numbers of talented, ambitious students who today are systematically lost to us, can together play a role in the reconstruction of democracy in America.

Resisting the Vocational versus Liberal Arts Dichotomy

One additional point bears emphasis here, especially as college in prison returns to the landscape of philanthropy and public policy. The first is the overworn distinction between vocational training and liberal learning. There are terrific pressures at work to push all American students into career-oriented training and to disparage both the spiritual, political, and practical benefits of liberal learning. I believe these pressures are misplaced and are often largely ideological rather than emprically based. The work of people like Peter Capelli, an expert at the Wharton School on the relationship between education and job markets, indicates that the gaps between targeted training and liberal learning lead to far fewer disparities measured by either rates of employment or earnings. But nowhere are the exaggerated pressures to extoll the benefits of training over learning likely to be greater than they are in prisons, and on incarcerated students. Most importantly, however, BPI's work suggests that the choice may be a false one. BPI has chosen not to choose between career training and liberal learning, but to integrate them. We have chosen to build career training tracks that follow from, and are rooted in, our ambitious liberal arts curricula. A track in public health, for example, integrates especially well with history and anthropology; the track in computer coding integrates with mathematics and analytic reasoning. We acknowledge the contemporary value of training, but also the practical skills that follow from rigorous liberal education. BPI's alumni out of prison have an employment rate between 60 percent and 80 percent: remarkable numbers for this group of adults. And BPI's alumni find work and flourish in a wide range of activities that reflect the full spectrum of opportunities and inclinations, rather than a predetermined narrowing of positions imposed upon them by prevailing low expectations. As noted elsewhere, alumni are working in trades and manufacturing, in social services and public health, in professions and the academy.

REPLICATION

Since 2010, BPI has worked with other colleges and universities, public and private, to replicate the successes we have had in New York. We have worked to expand novel ways for selective institutions to encounter highly capable students in unconventional places and times.

Through the Consortium for the Liberal Arts in Prison, we have cultivated faculty and administrators, developed new partnerships with state officials, issued seed grants, and provided intensive, long-term advice and technical assistance to new programs as we help design and implement them. Active in about a dozen states, BPI has helped launch and cultivate like-minded projects at Notre Dame University and Holy Cross College in Indiana; at Washington University in St Louis; at Marquette University in Milwaukee; at Wesleyan University in Connecticut; at Berea College in Kentucky; at Augsburg College in Minneapolis; at the University of Puget Sound in Tacoma, outside of Seattle, Washington; at Grinnell in Iowa and Goucher in Baltimore. Most notably, perhaps, these projects, based largely at private and selective liberal arts colleges and universities, are often forged in partnership with community colleges and public universities, including Minnesota State University–Mankato, Tacoma Community College, and Middlesex Community College in Connecticut. Such partnerships, between public and private schools, between two- and four-year colleges, were more common in American higher education a generation or two ago. Perhaps these new projects on college-in-prison are part of a broader return to such inclusive, and more fluid, ambitious, and democratic, academic alliances.

In each of these initiatives across the country, we have sought out academic institutions of prestige, financial power, and political resilience. Prestige is important in part because I think it helps disrupt the expectations, torpor, and bigotry of the prison space. It is not that less prestigious cannot, and don't already on occasion, offer important opportunities to people in prison. It is that the prestige of wealthier and more selective institutions is especially disruptive inside the prison, inspiring students and suffusing them over time with the belief in their own ability to transcend the poverty and indignity of their circumstances. This can, among other things, empower them to pursue a broader range of intellectual and creative challenges, even as they imagine and pursue more ambitious futures. The weight of the prison cannot be overestimated, and anything that helps displace it so constructively is a good thing. The financial power of these universities is important, because it enables them to meet prison and other state officials with a greater degree of independence. Not being reliant on the prison for most or all of their funding, they are in a better place to negotiate terms that serve the independence of the faculty and the best interests of their students. Their political resilience is essential in making them more attractive for some officials to partner with, and harder for others to expel once the college and university is established inside. The in-prison programs created by such universities, which are often "anchor institutions" in their city or region, can survive the ups and downs of political temper that might otherwise quickly kill public-sector projects.

In her work on college in prison Lagemann has emphasized the achivements of the California public university system. She has, quite rightly, placed that state's recent and very ambitious plan for education in prison, "Degrees of Success," in this historical perspective. California's renowned "Master Plan," implemented in the 1960s, resulted in what must surely be the world's most impressive democratic infrastructure for learning ever created. It built a three-tiered system that coordinated and integrated local community colleges, state universities, and public international flagship research centers. One of its most admirable strategic successes was to build a universal public system that embraced both "mass" and "elite" educational ambitions. These are treated as terms of art by sociologists of higher education like Martin Trow, and they refer not primarily to *who* studies, but to the institutional structures themselves. Here, then, "elite" refers to the attempts of the designers of the UC system to create exceptionally inclusive higher educational opportunity for all, while also creating avenues to participate at levels of the highest intensity and rigor in both undergraduate study and advanced graduate research.

In approaching the prison as site, I fear that few public systems of higher education have so ambitiously sought to integrate "mass" forms of inclusiveness and forms of study that are at once rigorous and integrating. If this tension, and indeed division, between mass and elite learning opportunity is a challenge for American higher education generally, nowhere is the challenge less likely to be met than in prison. The problem is that, when it comes to people in prison, or programs designed for them, this highest aspiration—to create structures at once inclusive and excellent that diversify rather than narrow the subjects of study and the roads of future intellectual and professional life—is rarely if ever identified as a goal.

This amounts to an all-too familiar bigotry of low ambitions. I fear that future innovations in college in prison will not be designed with such a truly democratic vision of excellence, of creeating networks that lead to both mass inclusion and the genuine facilitatation of the broadest and most ambitious opportunity. This is hard to do, and perhaps only the California system has achieved it; but it is even harder to do in prisons. Invoking "quality" is not enough—it's too easy to disagree about what that term means, and to invoke it as a hollow shibboleth. Instead, the proof of such democratic quality must be in the sorts of jobs, careers, intellectual and creative pursuits, and above all institutions of higher education, that participants continue on to afterward.

As indicated in chapter 1, and built into the strategies of how we have replicated our work through the Consortium, we have taken an approach that emphasizes the importance of private educational institutions of prestige, financial power, influential social networks, and political resilience. Public colleges and universities can play a similar role. But they may typically face greater obstacles, both to disrupting the preexisting culture and tenor of relationships with students in prison, and in creating inroads into the highest levels of professional and academic achievement afterward. For this to happen, the truly democratic ambitiom that includes both radically inclusive opportunity and the most rigorous creative production across all fields and disciplines, once aspired to in California, would have to be embraced anew.

CORE PRINCIPLES

A number of other core principles guide us and our partners in this work, many of which have been articulated well by my BPI colleague Jeff Jurgens. Among the most important of these is maintaining the utmost independence of the college in all aspects of its functioning inside the prison. This includes hiring the staff who represent and are entirely employed by the college, and, of course, selecting professors, who are paid by the college and are overwhelmingly, and at times exclusively, drawn from its tenured faculty.

The academic aspects of each program and its academic governance are entirely under the supervision of the college or university, rather than the departments of corrections with whom we partner. The first goal is to offer people in prison as full a college experience as possible, and not to educate conventional undergraduates, correctional staff, or to use the prison as a site for faculty research.

Each curriculum reflects the strengths and mission of its sponsoring college or university. At the same time, each program's courses are largely "institution-neutral," by which we mean that they are not centrally concerned with students' experiences as incarcerated people, or the facilities in which they are held. Such themes and topics may enter into the curriculum by way of faculty's preexisting or developing areas of expertise and research, or by way of students' own initiative, as individuals or collectively. But they are not established by the college as innovations specifically by or for its development of new programs for students in prison. A comprehensive commitment is made to weave remedial or developmental work into the very fabric of the full, broad, liberal arts training. While first-year students almost always begin with only a GED or its equivalent, they are engaged from the first as candidates for the institution's most ambitious four-year degrees, and curricula are developed backwards, so to speak, from this goal.

The work, then, requires maintaining a delicate balance between the independent college or university on the one hand and the prison officials who host it on the other. Substantial degrees of mutual respect and trust are obviously essential. The areas of closest cooperation must be attuned to the academic imperatives of the project. For us and our partners, these include some rather extraordinary levels of cooperation. In a most notable example, participating students are granted "educational holds" that allow stable, ongoing enrollment in a single campus inside a prison, which requires officials to resist other institutional imperatives associated with the classification and movement of people in and across prisons in the system. With such holds in place, a genuine campus, and a lasting community of students within the prison, can be developed. A long-term relationship between the college and its students who are enrolled while incarcerated must be established and maintained, which more or less goes against the grain of standard—and convenient—operating procedures within a prison's administrative system.

It is conceivable, and maybe even likely, that maintaining the college's intellectual and above all the administrative independence inside the prison will limit the scale of such activities. By most measures, it would certainly compromise its efficiency. But it is, in my view, essential.

The college that establishes itself inside the prison without disrupting the prison as experienced daily by its students inside has failed. A disturbance of the normal modes of operation is essential, as only this can lead to the alteration of the daily experience of the time and space of incarceration upon which everything envisioned and narrated here depends. If and when systematic opportunity of this kind returns to prisons in states across the country, a number of core principles of this kind are *essential*, if we wish to avoid simply expanding the realm of corrections, rather than finding in the prisons the countless people who, as students, represent a crucial strategic opportunity for American higher education.

Speaking in Confinement

For all of my ultimate optimism about the work of BPI, I try to remain critical and wary; sober about what's wrong, what's compromised, and even, to some degree, what's impossible about college in prison. Perhaps above all, I try to keep some perspective about the liberal arts in prison—about pursuing a genuinely emancipatory education under conditions of confinement.

I went in to Woodbourne to see Joseph a few days before he was due to be released. I had known him for just over ten years—from the first semester Bard had ever offered college in prison. We were a year apart in age.

I told him what my five-year-old son had said while we were reading *The Wind in the Willows*, when, during the courtroom scene, the child had interrupted my reading. He loved school, and was aware of my work at BPI in an early but vivid way.

"Daddy," he asked, "do the people who run the prison *want* *there* to be a school inside?"

Joseph responded to this anecdote by saying, "That's a very insightful question your little one has asked." We reminisced about our first class in 2001—reminding him of his essay exam on Henry Clay's Omnibus Bill of 1850 back when we first met ten years earlier.

I said goodbye, and that we'd meet soon.

After a pause, Joseph said: "Well, Daniel. Now you will meet me for the first time." Joseph, in his typical style—condensed, ironic—was drawing attention to the prison confines within which *all* of our conversations, our shared study, our work together over the years, had taken place.

We knew each other well, but only within that context, and in the shadow of that frame and under the forces it casts in all directions. Had we come to know each other well, working on a common project of such intensity, for so long? No doubt we had. But that knowledge too was determined, distorted, defined by the prison. And no amount of good faith, or critical reflection, or care on the part of a student, teacher, or a college, could control for that. There was another realm of truth on the other side, where not one of us, but both of us, were free.

LETTING GO

No doubt Joseph had long been preparing himself for the great challenge of being released after eighteen years in prison. The college had been one way he had built bridges to that future life. But now that he was about to assume it, he had to confront the great breach, the chasm that lay before him.

I end the book with the words of a formerly incarcerated person, now an accomplished poet and novelist, Easy Waters. Years ago, I heard him tell this story to an audience at Wesleyan University, where students were beginning to launch a college-in-prison program. He went to prison as an adolescent and had spent most of his youth inside. His first novel, *Streets of Rage*, was published in 2015.

As a teenager at Riker's Island, Easy began to read books, escaping into them as he waited for a transfer to a maximum-security prison upstate, where he was to spend the next twenty years. He recalled his mother's words then: "You can lose everything—possessions gained can always, always be taken away. But an education—nobody can ever take that from you."

At first his reading was like a drug; it was an escape. He read voraciously, unconsciously, indiscriminately. These words resonated to me as I listened to Easy tell this story about the passion of his reading, and his relentless, slow, fierce accumulation of books. I felt the power of that injunction toward an education that was the first among possessions, because it alone could not be taken away.

As he made his way upstate, and the years rolled on, he gradually became a serious reader. Already by that time an accomplished autodidact, he entered college in prison in its previous incarceration in New York. He thrived and completed a degree. All the while he continued to accumulate books. The prison had rules about how many books an inmate could keep in his cell—they limited him to twenty at a time. Easy spent many more years in prison after completing his BA and then MA degrees. All the while, he amassed more and more books. Having at first been a lifeline, a vein opened to another world in desperation, his books eventually became his world, an alternative architecture around him. Whenever he reached the quota of twenty volumes, he shipped the books home to his mother in Brooklyn.

Easy tells of his release, two college degrees and twenty years later, at the age of thirty-six. He returned to his mother's house, where she had kept every book, preserved every volume. The walls of their small row house were jammed, the basement also lined with shelves and overflowing with decades of books. They were the index of his appetite, his preservation, and of the quote inside his tiny cell miles away upstate. Thousands of volumes packed the house. What had been a mental and intellectual refuge in his life in prison was now hoarded at his boyhood home.

Overwhelmed upon his return, Easy wallowed in the house. After several weeks of languishing, something snapped. He awoke one morning and driven in a feverish dream-state, he descended to the basement and filled his arms with books. He began to carry them out of the house and pile them up on the street corner. Trip after trip. First his mother protested, then she tried to physically restrain him, and finally she watched, resigned, tearful, as he worked ceaselessly, silently, the entire day, and into the night. Over the course of an endless, frenetic day, a day without words, without stopping, he moved thousands of volumes by the armful, piling them upon the street corner to be taken away by the occasional passerby, to be hauled away in the trash.

Only then, he said, did he begin to resume his life.

Acknowledgments

This book has grown out of an institution invented, reinvented, and sustained by others, and is rooted in the achievements of talented and courageous students.

Nobody has inspired and supported me more in this endeavor than Laura Kunruether, my friend and loving companion of twenty-five years. She is a brilliant writer and anthropologist, and her way of thinking and seeing the world informed every aspect of my intellectual coming of age. Without her there would be nothing. Our sons Rafael Sylvan and Sascha Benjamin have had to put up with each of their parents' writing time away. Despite the absences caused by my selfish devotion to this project, they have always welcomed me back with open arms: I can only hope that some of their artful magic has made its way to these pages. As they have both recently noted: now there's more time to play. My beloved sister Tania, and Andrew, my old friend and brother by marriage, are artists and adults I admire: I continue to look to them both as models of how to live and how to work.

I owe a special debt of gratitude to Dhana Laxmi Hamal, whose undergraduate career at Bard and subsequent graduate studies in political science at the University of Toronto overlapped with most of the writing of this book. She is the wisest political person I know and, with her characteristic brilliance, she understands as well as anybody what BPI is all about. At once family and friend, she has instructed and encouraged me at every turn. I have tried to live up to her exacting standards, and remain, as always, in awe of her boundless personal courage.

Bard as an institution has nurtured the Prison Initiative as no other college would or could. I want to acknowledge the courage of President Leon Botstein, the early indulgences of Vice-President Robert Martin, and the sage forbearance of Dean Michèle Dominy, who first introduced me to BPI. For fifteen years the generosity and dedication of the Bard faculty has been unfathomable. Despite the omnipresent demands placed on them by the life of the college, they embraced BPI from the beginning as a natural part of their calling. BPI exists because of their work and is suffused with their ways of being in the world. Special thanks to those who have most shaped BPI, and hence how I understand the work: Daniel Berthold and Myra Armstead; Tabatha Ewing, Jeff Jurgens, Franz Kempf and Justus Rosenberg.

I'm indebted to Max Kenner, BPI's founder, who brought me into his work and has entrusted me with much, at many steps along the way. He has been an ally and friend for nearly two decades, and I continue to admire his unique *menschenkenntnis*. I'm also grateful to another of BPI's long-standing directors, Jed Tucker, with whom I cut my teeth at BPI and who brings so much wisdom and kindness to the work in New York and, increasingly, across the country. Also special thanks to the other directors who lead BPI and make it all that it is: Megan Callaghan, Delia Mellis, and Laura Liebman. I benefitted from many early conversations with Dorothy Albertini, and also recall with fondness the fearless and ebullient Anita Micossi—a teacher and advisor who fought tenaciously on behalf of every student. We lost her early and suddenly. The incomparable Ellen Lagemann has been magnanimous as a mentor, teacher, and friend. Few people of such remarkable accomplishment in this world are half as generous as she. I am proud to join the countless ranks of those whom she has supported at crucial moments in their professional lives. Finally, this book would not exist without the historian Peter Mickulas, senior editor at Rutgers, who took a chance on an untested author and an eccentric and often incoherent manuscript. His ability to balance intellect, idealism, and the reality principle made this project possible.

I have gained too much from too many students to recount: many of them were colleagues first and foremost. Yet I must thank especially Wesley Caines for the depth of his humanity, unbreakable self-possession, and his indomitable capacity for joy, as well as the brilliant Anibal Cortes—one of the best professors I've ever had the good fortune to study with. Erica Mateo continues to inspire with her wit, her ambitious love of life, and incisive mind. Of the many others whose insight and spirit have stayed with me from the beginning, special thanks to William Doane, Frank Fissette, Justice Walston, Jule Hall, Salih Israil, Derek Rawlings, and the late Miguel Santiago.

Several senior colleagues have taught me much by word and deed, and are busy transforming the landscape of American criminal justice: Glenn Martin at Just LeadershipUSA, Vivian Nixon at the College and Community Fellowship, and also Benay Rubinstein at Cornell and Jodi Lewen in Berkeley. More recently, Lul Tesfai, Jasmine Graves, and Jessica Neptune have given me faith in what comes next. Long ago, David Cohen and Martha Nussbaum each went out of their way to intervene in my life and save me from the University of Chicago winter. They opened the door for me, as it were, and then helped me walk through it. I remain indebted to each.

From near and far, several professionals in corrections have taught me much about how and why to do this work. Thanks especially to Linda Hollman, David Miller, the late Charles Pierra, and, above all, the incomparable Dr John Nally. Susan Tucker, a force to be reckoned with at the Open Society Institute in its formative decade, was a brilliant and early mentor; her brave support made BPI, and my involvement in it, come to life. The Reverend Steven Chinlund moved me deeply from my earliest days in this work, and his words continue to ring in my memory. As the Reverend Chinlund always said when blessing the power that inspires things like BPI: we know it by many different names, and by no name at all.

With tact and love, Howard Kunreuther has given me all the right advice at all the right times, and has supported this book in countless ways. Finally, I am profoundly grateful to Craig Wilder, who is as wise as he is generous. I look forward to continuing to learn from him, and have done my best to make the most of his invaluable critiques and support.

This book is dedicated to my parents, Joanne and Stephen, who transform the lives of all who enter their magic circle.

Whatever else this book may be, I hope it is a tribute to the courage and hard work of the students who have built BPI and who pass it on, as one part of their precious legacy, to others. May the works of the next generation come to fruition in our time, and in a very different place.

Selected Readings

THE READINGS BELOW are all from the courses that I have taught for BPI and out of which have grown the interactions with students depicted in this book. "The Constitution and Slavery" is the class behind chapter 2, which ends with the speech written by student Lloyd Adams about Frederick Douglass's autobiography. "Law and Literature: Dostoevsky's *Crime and Punishment*" is the class that frames chapter 3, and the discussions of moral freedom, social structure, and change. Finally, a course called "Civics," which is a critical look at the liberal tradition in America, underlies Noble's use of James Baldwin in preparing the speech he ultimately abandoned in preparing for our first graduation in chapter 4.

On Slavery and U.S. Constitutional History from the Founding to the Civil War

Douglass, Frederick. *Narrative of the Life of Frederick Douglass, An American Slave, Written by Himself.* Edited by William L. Andrews and William S. McFeely. New York: W. W. Norton, 1997.

Finkelman, Paul. *Slavery and the Founders: Race and Liberty in the Age of Jefferson.* 3rd ed. Armonk, NY: M. E. Sharpe, 2014.

Phillips, Wendell. *The Constitution: A Pro-Slavery Compact; or, Extracts from the Madison Papers, etc. selected by Wendell Phillips.* New York: American Anti-slavery Society, 1856.

Potter, David M. *The Impending Crisis, 1848–1861.* New York: Harper & Row, 1976.

On Mass Incarceration

Alexander, Michelle. *The New Jim Crow: Mass Incarceration in the Age of Colorblindness.* New York: The New Press, 2012.

Forman, James Jr. "Racial Critiques of Mass Incarceration: Beyond the New Jim Crow." *NYU Law Review* 87 (2012).

Garland, David. *Culture of Control: Crime and Social Order in Contemporary Society.* Chicago: University of Chicago Press, 2001.

Gottschalk, Marie. *Caught: The Prison State and the Lockdown of American Politics.* Princeton, NJ: Princeton University Press, 2015.

Mauer, Marc, and The Sentencing Project. *The Race to Incarcerate.* New York: The New Press, 1999.

Wacquant, Louïc. "Deadly Symbiosis: Rethinking Race and Imprisonment in 21st-Century America." *Boston Review* (April/May 2002).

On Dostoevsky's *Crime and Punishment*

Bakhtin, Mikhail. "The Hero's Monologic Discourse and Narrational Discourse in Dostoevsky's Early Novels." In *Fyodor Dostoevsky*, edited by Harold Bloom. Philadelphia: Chelsea House Publishers, 2003.

Fanger, Donald. "Apogee." In *Dostoevsky and Romantic Realism.* Cambridge, MA: Harvard University Press, 1967.

Frank, Joseph. *Dostoevsky: The Seeds of Revolt.* Princeton, NJ: Princeton University Press, 1976.

Lukacs, Georg. "Dostoevsky." Trans. René Welleck. https://www.marxists.org/archive/lukacs/works/1949/dostoyevsky.htm.

Zenkovsky, V.V. "Dostoevsky's Religious and Philosophical Views." In *Dostoevsky: A Collection of Critical Essays*, edited by René Wellek. Englewood Cliffs, NJ: Prentice-Hall, 1962

On "Civics" and the Liberal Tradition in America

Baldwin, James. "Many Thousands Gone." In *Notes of a Native Son.* Rev. ed. Boston: Beacon Press, 2012.

Du Bois, W.E.B. *The Black Reconstruction of Democracy in America, 1860–1880.* New York: The Free Press, 1998.

The Federalist Papers, No. 10 & No. 51. Edited by Terence Ball. Cambridge: Cambridge University Press, 2003.

Foner, Eric. "Introduction: The Idea of Free Labor in Nineteenth Century America." In *Free Soil, Free Labor, Free Men: The Ideology of the Republic Party Before the Civil War.* New York: Oxford University Press, 1995.

————. "Not All Freedom Is Made in America." Op-ed. *New York Times*, April 13, 2003.

Greenberg, Edward S. *The American Political System: A Radical Approach.* 5th ed. London: Longman, 1997

Hartz, Louis. *The Liberal Tradition in America.* San Diego: Harvest/HBJ, 1991.

Hofstadter, Richard. "The Founding Fathers: An Age of Realism." In *The American Political Tradition.* New York: Vintage, 1974.

Smith, Roger. "Beyond Tocqueville, Myrdal, and Hartz: The Multiple Traditions in America." *American Political Science Review* 87, no. 3 (September 1993).

Taylor, Charles. "Atomism." In *Philosophy and the Human Sciences: Philosophical Papers: 2.* Cambridge: Cambridge University Press, 1985.

————. "Hegel: History and Politics." In *Hegel*, reproduced in *Liberalism and Its Critics*, edited by Michael Sandel. New York: NYU Press, 1984.

Tocqueville, Alexis de. "Introduction," "Tyrrany of the Majority," and "On Individualism in Democratic Countries." In *Democracy in America.* Chicago: University of Chicago Press, 2000.

Note: The student speaker named Joseph draws on David Waldstreicher's *In the Midst of Perpetual Fêtes: The Making of American Nationalism, 1776–1820* (Chapel Hill: University of North Carolina Press, 1997) from a course entitled "Making National Citizens," created by Bard professor Myra Armstead.

Index

About the Author

Daniel B. Karpowitz is the director of Policy and Academics for the Bard Prison Initiative (BPI) and a lecturer in Law and the Humanities at Bard College. He has served as a faculty member, director, and leader of BPI since 2001. Karpowitz is co-founder of the Consortium for the Liberal Arts in Prison, an organization that launches and cultivates college-in-prison programs across the country, and he has written and spoken extensively on criminal justice and the benefits of higher education in prison. Prior to joining BPI, he had worked at the Lawyers' Committee on Civil Rights on residential segregation in Chicago, on alternatives to incarceration for young people in his native Philadelphia, and on race-based insurance underwriting in New York. He has taught in the Rhetoric Department of the University of California at Berkeley, was a Soros Justice Fellow at the Open Society Institute, a fellow at the National Endowment for the Humanities, and a Fulbright fellow in Kathmandu, Nepal. He holds a J.D. with Honors from the University of Chicago Law School, where he was a Public Interest Law fellow. He earned a B.A., Phi Beta Kappa, *summa cum laude*, from the University of Pennsylvania.